The Power of Things Unseen

THE
POWER
OF
THINGS
UNSEEN

Tales of Choosing Crazy Over Normal

Leanne R. Wood

NEW YORK

NASHVILLE • MELBOURNE • VANCOUVER

The Power of Things Unseen

Tales of Choosing Crazy Over Normal

Published in New York, New York, by Morgan James Publishing. Morgan James is a trademark of Morgan James, LLC. www.MorganJamesPublishing.com

The Morgan James Speakers Group can bring authors to your live event. For more information or to book an event visit The Morgan James Speakers Group at www.TheMorganJamesSpeakersGroup.com.

ISBN 9781683505259 paperback
ISBN 9781683505266 eBook
Library of Congress Control Number: 2017905339

Cover Design by:
Rachel Lopez
www.r2cdesign.com

Interior Design by:
Chris Treccani
www.3dogcreative.net

In an effort to support local communities, raise awareness and funds, Morgan James Publishing donates a percentage of all book sales for the life of each book to Habitat for Humanity Peninsula and Greater Williamsburg.

Get involved today! Visit
www.MorganJamesBuilds.com

For Murray,
And our beautiful daughters Victoria and Julia,
I will never stop loving you.

TABLE OF CONTENTS

. . . .

AUTHOR'S NOTE

. . . .

I never really intended to write a book. I stumbled upon it in a funny sort of way.

Whenever I regaled my long-suffering friends with a tale or two about one of my crazy escapades in Romania, they would inevitably tell me I should write a book. I sincerely thought they were nuts. Who would be interested in my story?

Two years ago I wrote a short blog celebrating the astounding fact that I had reached the thirty-year milestone in my marriage. Amazingly, we were still in love. Aware that a long lasting marriage doesn't happen easily, I candidly wrote about the joys and struggles, the love and angst, and the happy moments and dark times of our journey together. Still, I kept hearing: "You should write a book."

Slowly I began to realize that I did have a story to tell after all.

Before I knew it, my "writer floodgates" burst open. I would steal whatever spare time I could find in the day to write. Several hours would fly by and I would find my fingers still tapping away at the computer, my story pouring out of me. One day I looked up at my husband and said, "I think I'm writing a book." He smiled at me and said, "Of course you are."

So now, a year later, and here it is.

My story is about more than just my wild adventures as a young mother with no resources, gallivanting around the globe. My real story is about having courage to follow your inner voice and do what is written within you to do, no matter what. It is about stepping outside of "normal," when your gut tells you to. Time and again people tell me they want to take a new path, to branch out into something different, but they have so many reasons why they can't. My story is for those of you who need courage to step out and follow your dreams, even when they look impossible

My wish is that my tale will inspire you to take that "one next step" in front of you, even if you can see no further ahead. I want you to know that you don't have to follow a "normal" path if you feel your gut is telling you to do something else. I hope *The Power of Things Unseen* will give you the courage to listen to the whispers of your inner voice and do what is within you to do.

There are so many amazing people who have helped to make this book a reality. My gratitude to them knows no bounds. At the top of this list of heroes is my husband Murray. He has kept me going through the tough moments, encouraging me to keep writing even when I felt like throwing in the towel. He spent countless hours listening to my ideas, giving suggestions, and scrolling through my manuscript with a fine-toothed comb. He makes me laugh. He always believes in me. He is my rock.

My thanks to my daughters Victoria and Julia for letting me tell this tale. I am so thankful for all the fabulous adventures we had together. They are now beautiful women who continue to teach and amaze me. I am so proud of them both. I cherish their love not only as daughters but as close friends as well.

I am extremely grateful to my parents Dennis and Rowan. I wish my Dad were still here to read this story. He taught me to never give up and to always find the best in every situation. He was the most positive person I have ever known. My kind and gentle mother is still a constant source of love and support for me. I am so thankful for the wonderful upbringing full of love and opportunity that my parents selflessly gave me.

I would not have a story to tell without all the spectacular characters that I encountered on my journey. I am thankful to every one of them for agreeing to let me tell our tales. I love that all of our stories are interwoven and that we grow as we interact with each other. I particularly wish to thank my many dear Romanian friends. I am deeply grateful that they so warmly welcomed me to their beautiful country and taught me so much about gratitude and the true richness of life.

In writing this story I have relied only on my memories of the events I share. I have endeavored to keep my narrative as accurate as possible, while also using my creativity to tell the story. I am so thankful to my editor Justin Spizman for his patience and guidance. He helped me focus and find my voice. I am forever grateful to my team at Morgan James Publishing for giving me the opportunity to make my dream of publishing a book become a reality.

Leanne R Wood

CHAPTER 1

Crazy Woman and a Scotch, Please

H uge mounds of rubble loomed before me in every direction and I felt as if we were entering an abandoned bombsite. I struggled into the Otopeni Airport entryway, lugging our oversized suitcases with my two small daughters, Victoria and Julia, in tow. They had been instructed, no matter what, to keep a viselike-grip hold on my arms. They were doing such a fantastic job that both my hands were going numb from lack of blood flow. I was on full alert, aware that pickpockets and thieves were jostling closely around us, just waiting for me to become distracted and ignorantly offer up my treasures to their sticky fingers. We were on our own in a foreign country, and I still did not speak a lick of Romanian. Traffic to the airport had been horrendous, and we had little time to spare. Hence, our seven-hour journey to Bucharest had taken a whole lot longer than I had anticipated. I hated cutting things finely like this, so I endeavored to calm my jitters with one of my little peace mantras, which was really just an internal eyeroll and an inner berating of myself to not be so bloody fearful all of the time.

After elbowing my way through the unruly gaggle of waiting travelers, we finally made it to the check-in counter. There was no such thing as an orderly line here. I had shamelessly forced myself to the front as though I were one of those brazen and entitled American tourists who make us all cringe. You know the ones. They are usually wearing brightly colored terrycloth track suits or flowered shirts, and there is always a lot of big hair or comb-overs involved, gobs of sparkling jewelry twinkling brightly, and outrageously loud voices gabbing about nothing terribly interesting at all as they clamor to the front of the line. Well maybe I wasn't quite that bad, but I certainly came damn close.

Our time to get to the plane was running thin, and fear of an uncertain check-in procedure or worse still, of missing our plane, had made me act slightly ugly. I was not proud of my behavior, but there it was: With two children in hand, I relentlessly threw elbows at anyone within a two-feet radius. Finally, we made it to the front of the counter, and the agent handed us our boarding passes and relieved us of about a hundred pounds of luggage. We were waved forward to the security checkpoint. All seemed okay. We had made it. I could revert to my natural disposition of chill and sweet. Or so I thought.

"*Paşaport,*" the thickly accented security guard said.

We were traveling on our New Zealand passports, and I duly handed them over. We did not yet have British passports, but we did have permanent residency visas enabling us to reside in the United Kingdom.

"No good," the officer said.

I looked at him a little dazed. What was no good?

"*Paşaport* no good. Follow me."

"Um, excuse me, sir, but our plane leaves very soon. We need to go or we will miss it." I could hear the beginnings of a slightly annoying quiver in my voice, and my hands instinctively gripped tighter on to the two tiny hands holding mine. Fear, my old friend, quickly enveloped me.

The guard totally ignored me, took our passports, and stomped off, his gun bulging out of his hip pocket. It was quite clear that he was not about to have any more discussion with me. With no other options apparent, we scampered after him down a long corridor. He ushered us into a cramped, dark room with a single lightbulb hanging over a table with a chair. It felt like bad things had happened in this room. Instinctively, I shuddered. He immediately turned on his heel and exited the room, leaving the three of us stranded there alone. This did not feel good at all.

Even though I was scared shitless, I pretended to be calm as a cucumber for my girls' sake. Thankfully, they were not aware that anything was wrong. After all, they were only three and five years old, so how would they sense just how bad this could be? I chatted with them about quietly waiting. To distract them from my insanely elevated anxiety, I suggested they sit on the concrete floor and pull their Polly Pockets out of their miniature pink backpacks and play quietly while we waited for the "nice" man to return.

I nervously looked at my watch. We had exactly twenty minutes until takeoff. This didn't help my heart rate. Okay, perhaps it was time to practice some of those deep breathing relaxation techniques I had learned during my physiotherapy training. After an extremely anxious ten-minute wait, another guard, carrying a very menacing-looking machine gun, entered our dingy interrogation room. I let out a big sigh of relief, as I suspected this man was a supervisor and would surely sort out this apparent mix-up.

With passports in hand and broken English coming from his mouth, he explained to me that our visa stamps had expired because they only showed the date that we initially arrived to the UK. Since they were not multiple entry visas, he could not let us get on the flight because we would be turned away once we landed in the UK.

Thankfully, this was all a gigantic misunderstanding. I reached for our passports to show him that the stamps were actually permanent residency visas, which meant we could indeed reside in the UK and come and go as we liked. However, he ferociously shook his head, waved his finger menacingly in my face, pulled the passports from me, and walked out of the room. "Visa no good. Can't leave," he said. And with that, he slammed the door shut with a thud!

My mind raced. What the hell had just happened? Did he just say we couldn't leave? I tried to collect myself and look at my options. I thought, *Deep breaths, Leanne.*

In my slightly panicked brain, I deduced that these crooked agents likely just wanted a bribe from me before they would let us through to the waiting plane. After all, this was the early days of post-Communist Romania, where bribing still ran rampant. People were understandably attempting to claw their way out of the extreme poverty inflicted on them by their recently executed tyrannical leader. To that end, foreign money was like gold.

The only problem was that I only had twenty dollars left in my wallet, which I thought I really might need if we did not make it out of the country. I had given all my remaining money to my Romanian friend Dorin before saying goodbye to him when he dropped us off at the airport steps. It would be crazy to offer my last twenty dollars on a mere hunch that it could get the job done. I had no other form of currency or even a credit card.

I racked my brain for other options. It took all of one second to realize that I had none. My husband, Murray, was on the road somewhere between Romania and Scotland, and Dorin was heading back to Aiud. No one knew I was stuck here with two little kids and only twenty dollars in my wallet. I was most clearly in a pickle. It was now just five minutes until takeoff.

I tried to stay calm, but sheer panic was rising to newfound heights within me. I felt terribly alone and wretchedly afraid of being left behind. My thoughts started to head in horrific directions. In that moment of feeling totally trapped with no freaking options, my fight-or-flight mechanism kicked into full kick-ass gear.

"Pack up the Pollies," I said to the girls. "We're leaving!" Their little heads jerked up at me with wide eyes. Their tiny hands worked at record-breaking speed to put those beloved toys back into their backpacks. They were quite familiar with that *don't mess with me* voice from Mummy!

With massive amounts of adrenaline surging through my body, I helped them don their mini-backpacks, grabbed their tiny pink hands, and barged out of the room. We ran down the hallway that I had seen the guards amble down not so long ago, and I unabashedly started flinging open doors and looking into grimy rooms. The acrid smell of cigarette smoke and sounds of laughter finally led me to a room where all the guards were hanging out, nonchalantly having a smoke. I peeked in through a small window and could see they were ignoring my dilemma while they enjoyed a break from their day's hard work. How dare they do this to us. With fury and fear surging through my veins, I pushed open the door to their smoke-hazed hangout and forged right in. I could see our three passports and boarding passes lying hostage on a dirty little table hunkering in the corner.

Fear empowered me. Like a crazed woman, and at a decibel level that startled even me, I started yelling at them. "Those are our passports with legitimate UK entry stamps. You have no right to detain us."

Their response: total silence.

A wild woman with two tiny blonde girls carrying pink backpacks had probably never stood up to them like that before. The Romanian Securitate had created an environment of fear in which people cowered before authorities because boldly standing up for their rights could have invited a death sentence. And here I was shrieking like a banshee, driven by a mother's innate reflex to protect her babies and herself. I was completely outraged by the injustice of the situation, and my lack of control reflected this. The dam of my fury had suddenly burst wide open, and I let these power mongers know it. The guards were stunned into complete and utter immobility by what had just unfolded before their bleary eyes.

For a few seconds following my tirade, we locked eyes and stared at each other in complete silence. The cigarette fell right out of the machine gun bully's mouth and dropped onto the table. Quite honestly, I had amazed even myself, not to mention that the girls' eyes were almost popping right out of their baby heads. I had definitely surpassed the *don't mess with me* tone that they knew.

Before I realized what I was doing, I lunged for the three abandoned passports and boarding passes, snatched them off the table, grabbed the girls' hands, and took off running out the door. Poor little Victoria and Julia flew along beside me almost faster than their tiny toddler legs could carry them.

We kept moving forward, even though I was sure that I would hear machine gun fire popping behind us at any moment. I was terrified, but I also knew that something deep inside me, something beyond my normal reasoning, had made me the act the way I had. Now, there was no turning back. We just kept running until we found our boarding gate. It was unattended. I threw open a door, and we deliriously kept on running until we were outside on the tarmac. Our Tarom Airlines plane was right in front of us. We flew up the moveable stairs, just as the ground crew was getting ready to pull them away.

A most startled flight attendant with bright-purple, coiffed hair and exorbitant quantities of cleavage exploding from her uniform, looked at us as we burst through the door. I thrust our passports and boarding passes into her hands, gulping in great breaths of air. Sweat poured down my face.

"Welcome aboard," the wide-eyed woman said to us in stilted English while she scrutinized our documents.

"Are you alright, madam?" she asked. We were quite clearly a spectacle. She certainly had reason for concern. Puffing too hard to speak, I eagerly nodded. I did not want to draw any further attention to us than we were already doing. Any type of explanation would just complicate things.

"Everything looks in order here. Please quickly make your way to your seats. We are ready for takeoff." She handed our passports back to me.

Music to my ears! Maybe they hadn't yet called to tell her to detain us. I slowed down, took a deep breath, and told myself to walk calmly to our seats. The girls were staring up at me, stone quiet and quite perplexed by the clearly unmummylike shenanigans of the past few minutes. They were treading in unfamiliar territory.

Seconds later, as we belted up in our seats, we heard the whooshing sound of the plane door closing and the clank of the locking mechanism sliding into place. *Really?* I gulped another big breath of air and surreptitiously peeped down the aisle to make sure the door was indeed closed. Yes, it was definitely secured shut. I kept thinking that at any moment the door would pop back open and the police would come aboard and remove us. My mind was still in a frenzy and movielike flashes of firing squads flew around my addled brain.

I tried to control my hysteria, take some more big breaths, and keep up the façade that all was perfectly normal. I settled the girls into their seats as I continued to steal nervous looks toward the front of the aircraft. We just might be alright and not get shot for our earlier tirades. I could only think, *C'mon plane, please start taxiing!*

Minutes later, we heard the lovely roar of the engines. Soon, we were airborne. Sweet bliss!

I was shaking uncontrollably, however. I was replaying the last thirty minutes. They seemed like a horror film. They had been downright scary. My stomach churned as though I were adrift in high seas atop a tiny boat. I swallowed hard and shut my eyes while I endeavored to settle myself into some semblance of calm.

Suddenly, I heard the flight attendant beside me pulling me back to reality. She asked if I would like a drink. More music to my ears. *Yes,* I thought, *something very strong to settle my nerves would hit the spot.*

I looked at the flight attendant, smiled, and said, "Double Scotch please."

"I am sorry, ma'am, but we are out of Scotch for now."

"Oh, okay then, how about a gin and tonic?"

"We don't have that either."

"A glass of wine perhaps?"

"Sorry, no."

"Okay. What do you have?" I asked in a voice that had just shot up thirty decibels and was supplemented by a noticeable twitch in my left eye. At this point, just sniffing some alcoholic fumes would have been helpful.

"Well, today we have orange juice or water."

"Okay then. I would love some orange juice, please," I said, trying to be grateful, twitches growing stronger.

She paused and said, "Actually, we are out of orange juice today."

"Then water will be quite fine, thanks."

I started to laugh ever so softly, and then big tears streamed down my face. Suddenly, I felt overwhelmed by the relief of being on the plane with my babies safe beside me and having this absurd conversation about drinks with the flight attendant.

• • •

There is nothing like a "near-death" encounter to get you thinking. Yes, I know I was being ridiculously dramatic. There was no "beyond the light" experience likely to occur at the airport that day. And, of course, we were a long way from facing any firing squad. Even if the guards had made us miss our plane back to London, we would have eventually made it home in one piece.

As best I could, I lolled back into my creaky foam seat on the plane, which was winging its way back to Stansted Airport. Comfort was not the imperative design feature of this aircraft, and I wiggled to try and get settled. As I looked around, I noticed that the passenger load was very light. The plane was less than half-full. The back half of the aircraft was crammed to bursting with a frightening array of cargo. It was strapped into passenger seats and piled high in the aisles in a higgledy-piggledy manner, blocking access to the back of the plane. I sipped on my lukewarm water, hoping we would not need to make a speedy exit from the aircraft. *Silly speculation*, I whispered to myself. *Enough fearful thinking for today. Be still. Breathe.* Ah yes, it felt good to breathe.

Thankfully, the girls had fallen asleep, giving me time to further reflect. The events that had occurred in the airport just an hour before made me ponder my journey afresh. Not just this particular journey, but my life journey. Not just the reconnaissance trip to Romania that we had just completed, but the whole shebang. The journey that had led me, an ordinary kid from New Zealand, all the way to Europe, where I had met and eventually married a tall, skinny, extremely white Canadian named

Murray. Now here we were in Romania with our two little daughters, starting out on a whole new adventure. Something about this country had been written in our hearts. We knew it without a doubt. What a journey we were on! I thought about the fact that even though we were very normal everyday people, we had made some very abnormal decisions. We had thrown caution to the wind more than once and had found a way to overcome our fears and the apparent impossibilities that had faced us. Why had we done such things? Because we had decided to *do what was inside of us to do,* to follow our *inner voice* and take the next step in front of us, despite how foolish or terrifying it appeared. Amazingly, when we took these steps, we opened up our universe to miracles. We released amazing power. We had seen it time and again.

As I reclined in the plane seat that day, my thoughts migrated back through time. I found myself returning to my childhood in New Zealand. I pondered the all-powerful link that existed in my life, the link between following my intuition and overcoming the fears that blocked my way.

• • •

I had a pretty normal upbringing, considering it was the sixties and seventies, when most parents aspired to have Brady Bunch-like family dynamics. Of course that was quite the reach for any nontelevision script group of people, and almost every family I knew had oodles of dysfunction. But back then, that wasn't ever mentioned. My parents were very loving and gave the best of themselves to the monumental task of parenting. I was the youngest of four kids and was tolerated by my siblings most of the time, despite the fact that they considered me to be the spoiled baby of the family. This was totally not true from my perspective, but they would have none of my opinion.

From an early age, I had a fairly strong sense of right and wrong. Most kids possess a similar awareness. They are wired to please. Most of them yearn to fit in, to be a part of the crowd. They love to be accepted and praised. I learned early in life how this all worked. Do what was expected of me, and I would be affirmed and belong. Deviate from that, and there would be substantial consequences.

I didn't learn this from just one source, or at any particular time in my early years. I absorbed this message from every aspect of society and throughout every stage of my development. I just knew it did not pay to be too different or to venture too far out of the proverbial "normal box."

Somehow, I also learned to be afraid. I wasn't just afraid of monsters under the bed (which were frighteningly real to me at a young age), but I was afraid of doing wrong, of making mistakes, of letting people down, of dying and going to hell for being a bad person, of telling lies, of terrifying dreams, of being punished, for making wrong choices even when I thought I had made the right ones. My "fearful" list was frighteningly long. No one had taught me these fears. I had garnered them from sources far and wide and sequestered them deep inside me, holding them tight, and then making them my own.

I certainly don't blame anyone for the fear I cultivated in my early years. First, I have realized how idiotic it is to blame others for anything. But I also realized that no one intended for me to absorb this fear. I just took it on, soaked it up, and welcomed it deep inside of me.

In fact, I was lucky enough to grow up with really nothing at all to complain about. My dad was larger than life. He loved to have fun and had a mischievous streak, which made for an exciting childhood. He was a doctor with a very busy family medicine practice. Because Dad grew up in a fairly impoverished family, he took the responsibility of providing for us very seriously. Mum was a gentle, kind, and cultured woman. She was the stay-at-home parent, a constant in my life and a wonderful homemaker. There was no doubt that my parents did everything they could to give me a stellar start in life.

Each year, we took the most wonderful summer camping vacations. In the Southern Hemisphere, summer vacations begin at Christmas and go through January and into early February. The day after Christmas, we'd wake up at the crack of dawn and head north for our vacation spot on the beach, where we would set up camp and remain for the next four weeks.

When we arrived at our destination, a vacant quarter-acre lot set back from the beach, Dad would park our small airstream trailer in the optimum position. He had a set-up plan that would make any army general proud. Setting up our camping "compound" would begin posthaste and always spanned a full day. The trailer was the hub of all activity. It had a kitchenette, living and dining area, and it was also where Mum and Dad slept. Each of us four kids had our own separate tent "bedrooms."

Each vacation, my father erected his ingenious shower tent. He built a slatted wooden floor that kept us raised above the grass. He then added several poles that stood to just above head height, and he surrounded this structure with dark-green canvas. We then used a large immersion heater to boil water in a bucket. We'd carry the bucket of hot water over to the shower tent, where there was another bucket with holes in the bottom of it. We poured the hot water into the holey bucket, quickly hoisted it up with a pulley system, and clipped it into place above our head. *Voilà*, we had a shower. Water ran through the holes in the bucket at the ideal pace. To this day, I can still shower at lightning speed, much to my husband's amazement. You knew that when the bucket was empty, the soap had better be rinsed off because, ready or not, you were done.

There was also a toilet tent. Essentially, it was a long drop with a tent around it. Dad had located a private spot, dug a very deep hole with an auger, and then placed his homemade toilet box on top of the hole and surrounded it with the tent. The toilet was simply unforgettable. Made of wood and painted bright blue, the word "La-La's" was elegantly painted across it in large red letters. Dad had also painted a wooden sign emblazoned with the words "La-La's in Use." When nature called, the sign was hung on a nearby post to let everyone know not to come near. Dad had thought of everything!

There was an outdoor dishwashing table, again made by my jack-of-all-trades dad, with plastic wash and rinse buckets and a drying rack. Somehow Mum cooked large amounts of delicious food in the tiny kitchenette for the throng of people who came to our campsite for meals. Dad was always stationed in front of the barbecue, cooking mouthwatering mountains of meat to go with whatever delicacies Mum had made.

From a kid's perspective, it was all tremendous fun. For four weeks every year, this was our family home. Even the cat came with us on vacation. Evenings were a highlight. There was no TV. Every night was game night. Dad loved to play games, and over the years we had amassed a hoard of them. We all packed in around the tiny table in the trailer and played board game after board game after board game, while devouring unlimited supplies of chocolate and candies. I don't think Dad ever had family vacations as a child, so he was determined to make sure our vacations were as much fun as possible.

Dad and I were early risers. Every morning, just after sunrise, he sent me down the road to the little corner store for a newspaper. I was so excited to get up to run this errand because for those four weeks, he gave me extra money to get myself a treat. Inevitably, I came home eating ice cream or candies. It was an eight-year-old's dream breakfast for one sublime month each year.

Dad was never afraid to try something new. He always believed you could learn to do anything if you just set your mind to it. One day he decided we should have a sailboat for our summer vacations. He didn't have a clue how to sail, so he bought every book he could find on sailing, read up on it, and then set to. Before we knew it, we had all learned to sail. Soon enough, we were able to take the boat out on our own.

During a long day of sailing, my brother and I ventured miles across the water to explore new bays. Suddenly, we realized that the clouds had closed in and the wind was picking up substantially. It was time to head home. We ran back down to the beach, pulled the sailboat into the water, and set our sights on our beach several miles away. Within minutes, we realized that we had headed right into a very bad storm but we decided to push on. We were about halfway home when the storm turned ugly. Why had we not checked the weather forecast as we had been taught? Why had we not let our family know where we were headed?

Pelting rain lashed us, and the wind painfully whipped our bodies. We were wearing only our swimsuits and life jackets, and before long I was uncontrollably shaking and shivering, not just from cold but also from the terror of being out there in such a violent storm. Our hands and feet were numb, and it was almost impossible to hold on to the ropes as we tacked back and forth. We bobbed up and down like a tiny cork in the huge ocean swell. To prevent capsizing, we let the mainsail down and used only a partially raised small jib. The power of the wind and the ocean was truly alarming.

I genuinely thought we were going to die that day.

I don't know how long we were out in the storm, but it seemed like an eternity. My parents were frantic. They had no idea where we were. Sheets of precipitation pounded into the ocean, and there was almost no visibility. They knew we had gone out sailing early in the day, and now we had disappeared in a horrific storm.

I prayed like I had never prayed before. "Please don't let us drown. Please help us get back to shore alive." Somehow we did. As we approached land, we saw our parents and several of our friends drenched to the bone, standing on the beach in the thunder and lightning. They had been scanning the ocean with binoculars for hours, trying to locate our little red sailboat. I fell from the boat, limp with exhaustion from fighting the elements and my fear.

It was an event I will never forget. Even at such a young age, I knew just how lucky I was. I became aware in a way that I could not yet completely grasp that I was alive for a reason. There were things written inside of me that I needed to do. My *inner voice* was starting to whisper to me, even at this age.

CHAPTER 2

. . . .

One Second and Just a Few Inches Make a Difference

I reclined in my lumpy airline seat and sipped my highly unsatisfying, zero-alcohol, tepid water. Memories of my teenage years noodled around in my brain. You see, just as I had begun to hear my *inner voice* whisper to me as a child, that same voice became much louder in my teenage years.

Perhaps this was partly due to some momentous events that happened to me during these impressionable years. Since these events involved death or near-death experiences, they understandably pushed me to consider the meaning and purpose of life. They would help mold the direction I would choose to take as an adult.

New Zealand has very strict gun laws. Firearms were only legal for hunting, so we never saw guns on the streets. Even the police carried nothing more than a truncheon. I attended an all-girls boarding school as a day student. One wintry morning, a crazed man with a rifle came onto my school campus and hid in a crawl space under one of the buildings. As the boarding students poured out of the dining room after breakfast, he began randomly shooting at them. I had never heard a live gunshot before then, and I expect most of my school friends hadn't either. No one knew what was happening, so pandemonium ensued. Suddenly, one of my good friends fell to the ground and blood poured from her side. There were a few more loud pops, and then all was silent.

Sirens started to wail. The police swarmed the campus. We still had no idea what had happened. As paramedics rushed my friend to the hospital, her life hanging in the balance, the rest of us, all one thousand students, were corralled into the morning assembly hall. This type of event was so unheard of in New Zealand that no one considered the concept of a "shooter," nor that it would be dangerous to have all the students assembled in one place. It took the police several hours to find the shooter's body in the boarding house crawl space. He was identified as a suspect at large in the rape and murder case of a female hitchhiker he had allegedly picked up several weeks earlier. Allegedly, he was mentally ill and convinced that all females were his enemy.

When the police found his corpse, he was wearing army fatigues and carrying a stockpile of ammunition. I cannot begin to imagine how much more tragic that day would have been if he had not turned the gun on himself. Apart from the terror of the moment, the overwhelming imprint stamped on my thirteen-year-old's mind that horrible day was that human life is alarmingly fragile. I realized that everything can change within a split second. I did not know what would happen next in my life, but deep down I knew I wanted every moment to count.

Around the same time as the shooting, my best friend's seventeen-year-old brother died of cancer. I felt so totally unequipped to bring comfort to my friend. I wanted to have some answers for her but could find none. I felt so out of my depth. Death had robbed her of her brother. Why?

Next, I twice encountered one of humanity's worst tragedies: suicide. A very close friend's teenage brother took his own life. I spent a lot of time at my friend's house after the suicide. I tried to comfort her and do what I could to help around the home with the guests who visited to offer their condolences. Her mother's anguish was so great that she could not even stand up. It was the first time I had seen a completely broken human being. It frightened me. I could not comprehend the immense pain inflicted upon the family, nor could I understand the depth of suffering that would cause someone to take his or her own life. My friend's brother's death rocked me to the core.

Shortly after this, one of my classmates also committed suicide. Again, in despair, I questioned why some people could not make it through to the next day. What had made her so afraid to live? I wept for these peers who had left us. I felt sure there should have been a way out, perhaps even a balm for their sorrows. I was convinced that there were answers that could have prevented them from snuffing out their own lives. I wanted to find those answers. I wanted life to mean something.

Not long after these tragic suicides, I was in a serious hit-and-run car accident. A drunk driver hurtled through a stop sign and hit the car in which I was a passenger. Our car somersaulted several times and landed with a severe impact. I clearly remember thinking that I was going to die. I saw my life flash by in slow motion as the car spun out of control. To this day, I can vividly picture the moment when everything stood still and I so clearly thought, *My life is over.* Astonishingly the spinning stopped, leaving our car lying upside down in the middle of the road. In a daze, the driver and I crawled out. We were covered in glass and scratches but otherwise unscathed. When we surveyed the vehicle, it was obvious that the oncoming car had hit our car mere inches behind where I had been sitting. Miraculously, I was not only alive, but I was still standing. It dawned on me that a one-second difference would most probably have resulted in serious injury or perhaps even my death. I could not stop shaking uncontrollably at this thought.

Almost losing my life in this fashion and being involved with others who did lose their precious lives gave me an extraordinary perspective that I would carry throughout the rest of my life. I believed there could be joy and hope and fulfillment in life. A message was formulating within me. I wanted to yell to the world that each one of us has a reason to live.

• • •

Like I did, most teens face moments that push them to think about the meaning of life. No matter how dissimilar one's teenage experience is, it remains a time when we develop an understanding of who we are and what we want to become. I do not believe I am alone in finding that even at this young stage in life, I heard an *inner voice* speaking to me. During my teen years, I also discovered another marvelous truth: Humans are deeply interconnected. We are here to help each other. As I headed to college, this truth percolated inside me. I was privileged to live in a country that afforded great opportunity and freedom to its residents. I was lucky to have grown up surrounded by love. I had the wonderful advantage of continuing onto higher education. I knew I had been given so much, and I wanted to give back. I had no idea how that would unfold, but I felt it deep within me.

My college years were so much fun. My thinking was challenged, and I opened my mind to concepts that were very different from those with which I was raised. I fell in and out of love more than a few times and went through a devastatingly sad broken engagement that left a painful hole in my heart. By the time I had graduated from college with a degree in physical therapy and accumulated a couple of years work experience, I was ready for change. I could not see myself staying in New Zealand in the traditional routine of a nine-to-five job. There was a great big world out there, and I could feel it beckoning. It was time to spread my wings and fly.

So, at the age of twenty-three, I booked a one-way ticket to Switzerland. I had learned of a six-month multicultural training program with an international, interdenominational Christian nonprofit. Three months of the program involved traveling through and camping in Europe and the Middle East with other twentysomethings from all around the world. It sounded like fun and right up my alley. I had no idea what I would do after the six-month program, but I was confident something would open up for me. I started down a road that would transform my life forever, but at the time I did not even realize it.

My life journey would unfold with multiple twists and turns. I had no idea of the lessons I would learn nor of the paths I would take. There would be moments of prosperity chased away by total loss. My expedition would span numerous continents and take me to unfamiliar countries and cultures. I would know heartbreak followed by laughter and dark times eclipsed by bright moments. I would feel very alone and afraid, and I would be courageous and brave all at the same time. But one thing would stay constant throughout this life adventure: I would learn to listen to my *inner voice* and do what I knew was inside of me to do, no matter what the perceived consequences were. This alone would bring me freedom and meaning.

CHAPTER 3

· · · · · · · · · · · · · · · · · ·

Magic Mail and Diamonds

I arrived in Lausanne, Switzerland, chock-full of youthful anticipation. I brimmed with excitement about the adventures that I expected would unfold. I loved meeting people from all walks of life and from all four corners of the planet. This fed my soul and filled my "can't get enough of people reservoir" to overflowing. It was pure Leanne heaven.

One of the people I met on my new journey was an unassuming Canadian named Murray. I still remember the first thing I said to him: "You are the whitest human being I have ever met!" The words tumbled out of my unguarded mouth in a hot second. It was an absurdly true statement. He was from a fly-in town in the far north of Canada, with little sun, as evidenced by his incandescent white skin. But it was not the sort of thing that you say to someone when you first meet them.

I started to blush for saying something quite silly to a total stranger, one who I would be spending the next six months with. I gave myself another of my internal eyerolls and an inner berating for being such a bloody nitwit.

Thankfully, Murray had a wicked sense of humor. He lifted his sweater and flashed his pure-white Canadian belly, and we both chuckled at the absurdity of this first introduction. Unbeknownst to me, I had just met the amazing man I would marry a year and a half later. However, there was no love at first sight, partly because I was blinded by just how white he was. Over the next few months, we became great friends. We'd often find ourselves together, exploring new places on our travels across Europe. I loved his sense of humor and kind demeanor. I enjoyed hanging out with him as part of my new group of friends. We found ourselves running across Venetian bridges together while marveling at the beauty of the great city we were in. I managed to horrify him by my cruel bartering techniques with local artisans as we trolled through the underground markets in Istanbul.

We were a formidable team, and our friends crowned us the victors in our horseplay shoulder fights atop the travertine terraces of the thermal pools of Pamukkale. We climbed Masada together in 105°F conditions, and I tingled all over when he finally grabbed my hand and hoisted my puffing frame up those final few unmanageable feet to the top. He bought me gin and tonics on our ferry crossing to Crete, let me win at arm wrestles on a beach in Athens, and humored me with silly baked bean fart jokes that made me laugh because they were so ridiculous.

At the end of our six-month program, Murray headed back to Canada to continue his university studies. I had signed up to work with a nonprofit on an inner-city project in Dublin. We had no idea if we would ever see each other again. But something inside me was bubbling. I had most clearly been falling in love with this man over the past few months, so when his parting words were "Come and visit me in Canada," I knew I would do just that.

We wrote letters to one another for the next year. Mine were page upon page of flowing words about my daily activities and people I met while working and living in Dublin. He would reply with one page of succinct sentences from which I gleaned absolutely nothing. He was a man of few words, and I had no idea if he had any interest in me at all. I was ridiculous. I read each letter at least a hundred times, hoping to transform his short sentences into deep proclamations of his undying love for me. But no matter how hard I tried, I couldn't find a single jot of evidence that he had feelings for me.

Then, a letter arrived one day. It was an invitation from Murray to visit him in Canada. After reading it, I began an involuntary jiglike dance for the next hour, much to the amusement of my long-suffering roommate. She was well versed in the Murray-Leanne-maybe-love-affair saga. I wanted to visit him so badly, but no matter how creatively I looked at the possibility, I had no way of getting from Dublin to Canada anytime soon. I had no financial resources at all. I had spent every last cent on my training program and travel. I was a full-time volunteer for a nonprofit, and I was living on a shoestring budget. Quite simply, I did not have the resources to purchase an airline ticket to anywhere, not to mention Canada.

And this is where the miracles began to happen. I knew deep inside that I needed to do something but didn't have the necessary means to make it happen. This was when things beyond my power began to manifest.

I put it out to the universe that if I was meant to visit Murray, I would find a way to make this trip.

A few weeks later, I visited a friend who had badly injured her back and had been put on bed rest. As we chatted, she told me that she had an airline ticket to go with a group of friends from London to Los

Angeles to attend the LA Olympics. She was meant to leave in a few days. Unfortunately, her injury had left her bedridden, and there was no way she would make the trip.

"Would you like my ticket?" she asked me totally out of the blue. Was she freaking kidding me? "I can't get it refunded and can't use it, so I would love for you to have it. I planned to stay with some friends in LA, and I know you could stay with them if you want to," she continued as my excitement meter just shot off the charts.

"I would love your ticket!" came my exhilarated response. Who wouldn't want a free airline ticket to LA? I jabbered out my story about Murray's invitation to visit him in Canada. I explained that I did not have the money to purchase a ticket. I knew this kind gift from my friend was my first step to visit Murray. She was lying on her back in pain but was truly happy that her ailment would give me the opportunity to get to LA and maybe even to Canada.

"You have three weeks," she said with a twinkle in her eye, despite her debilitating back pain. "So find a way to get from LA to Canada and make it count!" I twirled out of her bedroom pinching myself with disbelief. How phantasmagorical was that! I suddenly had a way to get to the continent where Murray lived! Something magical was happening.

Now all I had to work out was how I was going to get to London from Dublin, and then how I was going to get to Canada from LA, with no money to do so. I had just over a week before I was due to leave and not a penny left to my name. If that wasn't enough, I had another minor problem to overcome.

Murray's last letter had revealed he would be moving but that he did not yet have a new address. He wrote that he'd send me a letter once he had it. Even worse, I had no phone number for him. There was certainly no Internet or email in 1984.

As I took stock of the situation, I summed it up like this: I lived in Ireland; I had a ticket from London to LA; Murray lived somewhere in

Canada; and at this point I had no way of knowing where he was, nor how to contact him. I just had to hope a letter with his contact details would arrive in the next few days.

Hmm. I'd have to overcome some hurdles to meet him, yet something deep inside kept telling me that it would all work out. Just take one step at a time. I would see things unfold. My heart kept doing that delightful skippity-skip thing it seemed to do every time I envisioned seeing Murray again. Getting this air ticket was the first thrilling development. I was quite sure of this.

It was time to fill in the gaps. The cheapest way to get to London from Dublin was by ferry to Holyhead in Wales and then by bus to the city. I called up a good friend who lived in London and asked if I could come and stay the night with her prior to flying out to LA. I checked the ferry schedule, packed my bag, and waited to begin my journey.

The days slowly trickled by. My heart began to sink. I had run out of time. I had to be in London the next day so I could make the flight to LA. The ferry departed at seven thirty the next morning, and I still didn't have the money to buy a ticket. I did not have a credit card, and I could not see a way to make it work. *What had I been thinking? Was I crazy?* I asked myself not for the first time in my life.

I lived in a large house with a group of people who worked for the same nonprofit organization as I did. We often ran programs for teens and hosted many events at the house. That afternoon while I was meeting with a young Irish girl I had been helping through some difficult situations, I heard the mail slot in the front door flap open and close. It was around three thirty in the afternoon, and there lying on the floor in front of the door was a single letter from my sister in New Zealand. I tore it open, and a money order fluttered out. Never had she sent me money. Even more astounding, the money order was for the exact amount I needed for my return ferry and bus tickets to London!

My heart pounded, and I whooped and hollered as I took off out the door for the ferry building with a stop along the way to cash the money order. As I sat on the bus that would take me to the bank, I looked at the date stamp on the letter. It showed today's date! Even though New Zealand is twelve hours ahead of Ireland, it seemed that it was physically impossible for that letter to arrive so quickly. The flight time from Auckland to Dublin, with stops, was at least twenty-seven hours. This realization blew me away. I swallowed hard as I felt emotion well up deep inside me. A power greater than me was working on my behalf, and I was holding a miracle in my shaking hands.

I arrived at the bank exactly two minutes prior to closing and cashed the check. Talk about cutting things close. Like a speedball, I then ran all the way to the ferry building and breathlessly purchased my ticket for the early morning sailing. I could hardly believe what had just happened. I was on my way to North America! I squealed, did a couple of very silly Michael Jackson-like moonwalk moves, and then realized that every eye in the Dublin ferry terminal was fixed on me. I didn't care how silly I looked, because I would indeed be on that seven thirty ferry sailing to London the very next morning.

Late the following evening, I sat in my friend's flat in London, sipping a cup of English Breakfast tea while excitedly recounting the story of my adventure. When I told her I did not know how to get in contact with Murray, she announced emphatically, "Well, we just need to find him, that is all!"

Her suggestion stopped me midsentence. "Of course I need to," I said. "But how? I was hoping to get a letter from him before I left Dublin, but nothing arrived."

"Let's get to work on this," she said as we summoned all of our sleuthing powers and analyzed the situation. It was fun to have an old friend from my teenage years help me plan this "Leanne meets Murray again enterprise." I gave her a massive hug, squeezing the air right out of her lungs. I executed a perfect little jig around her living room, and we roared with laughter, as girls on a mission together do.

Somewhere in the recesses of my brain, I thought I remembered Murray mentioning his father's name was Robert. We decided to check whether a Robert Wood who lived in the province of Saskatchewan had a son named Murray. Prior to the Internet, finding someone in another country was no easy feat. We called up international directory for Canada and asked for the phone numbers of all the Wood listings in Saskatchewan. Slowly, we began to work our way through the list, calling them all and asking them if they knew a Robert or Murray. Wood was a surprisingly common name.

It was well into the wee hours of the morning, London time, when we finally found his father. Yes, he confirmed, he had a son named Murray and he was in the process of moving. He would be visiting at his father's house in a few days, and I could call back then and speak to him. I hugged my friend about a hundred times and finally fell into bed for a couple of hours. Tomorrow I would be on my way to America!

· · ·

My first trip to LA was so much fun. It was enthralling to experience a city in the midst of hosting the Olympics. I explored as much as I could by bus and on foot. The family my friend had planned to stay with hosted me, so even my accommodation was taken care of during those first two weeks.

Finally, the long-awaited day came when I could reconnect with Murray by phone. I had stockpiled a fistful of quarters and found a nearby payphone. Breathlessly, I dialed his number.

"Hi," I said. "I'm in LA." I explained to him how I had arrived there. "Does your offer to come and visit this summer still stand? It would be amazing to see you again." My heart was somersaulting out of my chest, and my voice sounded strangely squeaky. *Settle down, Leanne*, I thought as I blathered on. "I am not sure how I will get there, but I have a couple more weeks in North America before I need to fly back to London, and I would love to see you."

As my coins quickly disappeared, we established that I should fly to Edmonton. Silently, I let out a proverbial "phew," delighted that he still wanted to see me. A good friend of ours, whom we had met in Switzerland, was getting married in Edmonton the following weekend. We would surprise him by showing up at his wedding.

"Would that work okay?" Murray gently asked me.

"Sounds great," I calmly answered, but my insides were still yipping with pleasure at the thought of seeing him again, and I wanted to yell, "That sounds AMAZING" at fever pitch!

As I hung up the phone, I was acutely aware of my continued lack of resources. I had no idea how I would purchase a return airline ticket to Edmonton. But I knew the next stop: travel agent. I hotfooted it to the closest one I could find. I put a ticket on a forty-eight-hour hold and boldly told the agent that I would be back within the next two days to purchase it. The miracles that had taken place so far had empowered me. All I could do was wait and pray. What happened next was truly fantastic.

Two days later, I was sitting on a bus in LA and in my normal friendly manner, I started chatting with the young woman sitting next to me. She was on vacation in LA, visiting from South Africa. Our chatter lulled for a few minutes, and then she unexpectedly turned to me and said, "Can I ask you a kind of strange question?"

"Of course," I said without a clue about what she was going to say next.

"Would I be able to give you a gift of money?" she asked. My mouth dropped wide open in astonishment. I made a strange grunting sound. Undeterred, she explained that just prior to departing on her trip, a friend had turned up at her home with an envelope full of American dollars. Her friend had asked her to take the money to LA and to give it to someone she would meet along the way. She didn't know who or why, but just that it was what she was meant to do.

"When you sat down on the bus beside me, I just knew you were the person," she said. "I don't know why, because you don't look like you need money, but I know that for some reason you do need some money, so here it is." She handed me a slightly crumpled envelope stuffed full of American dollars.

As anyone who knows me will confirm, I am rarely at a loss for words. But at that moment, I was speechless. Overwhelmed, big tears welled up in my eyes and rolled down my cheeks as I reached to hug her. I finally found the words to tell this stranger why I needed the money. I asked her to please thank her angel friend in South Africa for doing something strange and selfless, for acting upon a feeling.

It was awesome to realize that someone in South Africa I had never met, and most probably would never meet, had just given me a way to follow my heart and visit Murray. It was a truly staggering example of how we are all connected, right across the world. It was also a life-changing lesson for me about following your inner guidance, even when you have no idea why or how.

I arrived at the travel agent just minutes before the hold on my ticket would expire, and I handed over the cash with a ridiculously dramatic flourish. The tired looking person on the other side of the counter looked at me askance. *Fruitcake!* is what I imagined she was thinking. I didn't care one whit whether she believed I was loony, because I had just purchased the ticket that would change my life forever. I would leave LA two days later to visit Murray for a week. It had been a year since I had last seen him, and I recognized that my excitement level had just reached a ten on the Richter scale.

. . .

There he was!

I ran through the security gates and into the terminal to be greeted with a huge, warm hug and a lovely bunch of flowers. I tried to act normally and quell my elation at seeing Murray again, but that didn't work. I may have twirled and skipped. I definitely giggled in a ludicrously girly manner. Amazingly, he didn't seem to be fazed in the slightest. In fact, he appeared to be hugely delighted to see me again as well.

Murray had arranged for us to stay with family friends who were living in Edmonton. We stayed up all night chatting and recapping the last year of our lives. I did not sleep one wink that night. Sitting in a stranger's home in Edmonton, chatting to Murray all night long, waiting to attend our friend's wedding the next day—it was all so surreal. And it was pure joy.

Of course there is nothing like a wedding to make one think about getting married! The following night, after the wedding, Murray turned to me and said, "Do you think we should get married?" and without a second thought I said resoundingly, "Yes!"

We had not even dated, and we had just decided to get married. There was not a moment's hesitation. This kind, gentle, funny, and slightly awkward man, who had zero dress sense, was the person I wanted to spend the rest of my life with. I just knew this was the right decision, and so we decided to get engaged right there and then.

Murray quietly explained that he had used all of his savings on his previous year of university studies and that he did not have the money to buy me an engagement ring. Neither of us had planned this engagement. Even though I am a girly girl and love all things sparkly, I told him that it was okay. I was just so happy with all that had happened within the last few days. I did not need a ring. In fact, I still had not stopped my ridiculous twirling.

On my last day in Canada, Murray took me to look at engagement rings so he'd know what to buy when he had the financial means. After a leisurely, romantic afternoon of perusing jewelry stores, we found a beauty of a ring that he promised he would soon purchase

Murray then explained that we had one final stop before he would drop me off at the airport. He wanted me to meet some very close friends and tell them our happy news. With much joy, laughter, and, of course, some massive Canadian bear hugs, we shared the news of our engagement. We stayed for dinner. Before long it was time to get on the road and head to the airport. We were off after our goodbyes and more Canadian bear hugs.

The next thing I knew, Murray was pulling back into the parking lot of the jewelry store we had visited earlier that day.

"Why are we here again?" I asked, a little perplexed.

"We have an engagement ring to pick up," he said with a massive smile splitting his handsome face in two.

"Whaaaat?" It came out as something that resembled a bleating sheep noise, but thankfully Murray didn't seem to notice. The next amazing story quietly tumbled out from his lovely lips.

Earlier that day, Murray's friend Gary was at the office when in walked a client for whom Gary had done some pro bono work. With much gratitude, the client told Gary how things in his life had turned around for the better. He couldn't forget Gary's kindness and his help through difficult times. To that end, he insisted on paying Gary for the work he had previously performed.

Immediately, Gary knew the money was not for him. He had a strong feeling that when he arrived home, someone would be there who would need that money. Then Murray and I turned up quite unexpectedly for a last-minute meet and greet. Gary had known nothing about Murray's current financial state, but he knew that the money was meant for Murray. During a quiet huddle in the kitchen corner, Gary had given

Murray the money his client had given him. Murray had desperately wanted to buy me an engagement ring before I flew out that day. He hadn't known how to do that, but now here was his answer!

We arrived at the store only to find that the storeowner had reduced the price of the ring I had fallen in love with just a few hours earlier. Murray had the exact amount he needed to buy me the ring. I pirouetted out of the store, feeling like I might just explode from happiness. I had said I didn't mind not having a ring, but deep down I knew I would love one. I am, after all, a girl! And somehow, after my first disastrous engagement had fallen apart, a ring on my finger strangely made me feel just a little bit more secure about my betrothal to this gentle giant.

A few hours later, I was on the plane winging my way back to LA to continue my journey to Heathrow and back to Dublin. I was sporting a lovely sparkly ring and shamelessly flashed it around to anyone who cared to notice. My heart was full. What an astounding and truly spectacular trip it had been. What had seemed impossible just a few weeks earlier had in fact turned out to be wonderfully possible. I had listened to my *inner voice* and taken that one next step. Miracles had unfolded moments before I needed them. I had known the *power of things unseen*.

To this day, I go back to this story time and again. It reminds me to believe even when I can't see a way ahead. In times when I am unsure, when everything is unclear to me, when I feel wobbly inside, I take great courage from this amazing episode in my life.

I don't believe that miraculous happenings are only available for a chosen few. Not one of us is more special than another or deserves miracles more than another. Miracles are there for everyone, but often we only see them when we put ourselves on a path that requires miraculous intervention. Don't rule anything out because it seems impossible. Nothing is impossible. Expect miracles where there are blocks to you moving forward. Do what you know is inside of you to do. Follow your *inner voice*.

CHAPTER 4

. . . .

A Perfect Storm and a
Trip to Paradise

Three months after Murray and I became engaged, I completed my nonprofit job in Ireland and flew back to Canada to meet up with my groom. From there, Murray and I headed to New Zealand for our nuptials. We got married in the summer of 1985 (February in New Zealand) at a time when the weather was supposed to be stunningly gorgeous. But that wasn't the case. A severe tropical storm rolled in the day before our wedding, bringing with it terrific thunderstorms in place of the blissful and gentle sunshine we had anticipated. The storms were so severe that most of my hometown experienced extreme flooding and hours of power outages.

I was convinced the dire weather would ruin my perfect wedding day. As I watched the rain pelting against the windows and the lightning flashing across the thundering skies, my vision of a fairytale wedding diminished before my eyes. Instantly, I took on the role of the emotional bride and started the day in floods of tears to match the floods of raindrops. While I was being ridiculously dramatic over a storm, I just couldn't help myself. I chided myself to buck up, but to no avail. I couldn't quell the full force of my waterworks.

But of course, the calm, sensible, and unflappable Murray came to my rescue. He overlooked my distraught early morning sobbing, and in his calm, lovely way said, "Life is not perfect, Leanne, so let's just enjoy the day and make it a perfect one for us." He followed this statement with a very unseemly joke that magically turned my tears to laughter in a split second. I was a pushover when he cracked his stupid jokes, and for not the first time I thought, Yes, he is the perfect person for me.

The outdoor reception at my friend's beautiful vineyard was no longer viable, so we had to move the wedding indoors. We all crammed into a tiny candlelit room, but it didn't matter. I was crazy in love with a most remarkable person and had just agreed to spend the rest of my life with him. I was signing up for a lifetime of ludicrous witticisms and couldn't be happier with my decision. I had nothing in the world to cry about, and everything in the world to rejoice over. In its own rainy way, when absolutely nothing went as planned, my wedding turned out to be perfect.

But the storm had yet more in store for us. The rain that had deluged our wedding day morphed into a severe tropical cyclone. It whirled its way to the nearby Fiji islands, prompting all tourists to evacuate. Two days after the cyclone passed, we heard that there were incredible deals being offered to lure people back to the empty resorts. We were due to fly out the next day. We got on the phone and secured a one-week stay on an almost deserted Fijian island for mere pennies. We changed our return tickets to Canada, to include a stopover in Fiji, free of charge. Even if we had spent months planning it, we could not have planned a more wonderful and romantic honeymoon. We marveled at how truly amazing it was. The rain had indeed turned to sunshine for us. However, this sunshine adventure commenced with a slightly amusing episode. Let me explain.

We arrived at Nadi International Airport and discovered that the transportation to our resort island was a four-seater plane. Our jovial Fijian attendant pointed us to a puddle-jumper in the distance.

"You mean we need to walk across the tarmac?" I asked a little tentatively. It did not appear a wise thing to do, as planes were taxiing back and forth across our path to the plane.

After a reassuring nod from the attendant, we loped off across the tarmac, dodging incoming aircraft. We lugged our four massive suitcases full of wedding gifts to the plane. This plane looked pretty rickety. I mentioned this to Murray, but he said I had nothing to worry about. He assured me that he had taken lots of flights in all sorts of bush planes that looked just like this one. Murray had grown up in a very remote town in the far north of Canada where the only way in or out was by plane. There was an exception to this, however. For a couple of weeks a year in the depths of winter, when the weather often reached -40°C, an ice road was plowed fifty miles across a frozen snow-covered lake, allowing passage for trucks and a few brave souls who dared to cross it in their cars. Think Ice Truckers reality TV show and you get the idea. He then recounted a trip in a plane with a broken back window, when a hunting party tried to load up a moose and they accidentally stuck its hoof through the window. This was not the most reassuring story to hear when I was already feeling nervous! He assured me that this plane looked fine. I still was not convinced and did a little eyeroll at him, which he returned with a big, kind smile.

No one was around, so we just stood there beside the suspect-looking little plane, our gargantuan suitcases beside us. Planes buzzed all around us. "So much for safety regulations!" I muttered a little ungraciously. Murray slightly raised his left eyebrow at my muttering, but he just kept assuring me that all would be okay.

After a considerable wait, a big burly Fijian, wearing a skirt and slowly pulling a huge cart loaded with boxes, ambled over.

"Things have been disrupted by the cyclone, so we are taking some fresh supplies out to the island in your passenger plane," he said. "We don't normally fit supplies in with passengers, but today we have to or there won't be enough food on the island. A few of the other planes are out of commission due to the cyclone. It may be a bit tight in there, but it is a very short flight, so you should be okay." I looked at all the crates and boxes, our luggage, and then at the space behind our seats. My eyes bulged. There was no way he would fit all that into the little plane. I harrumphed. Murray shot me a sideways "calm down" look. I harrumphed again.

The man gestured for us to take our seats behind the pilot's seat. Then he loaded our overweight suitcases behind us and box after box of supplies beside our suitcases. There were crates of bananas, taro root, sweet potatoes, pineapples, and who knows what else. He just kept cramming stuff in. Unbelievably, he got every single one of those boxes into the little space beside our monstrous suitcases. He was a packing genius. His job complete, he said goodbye and assured us that the pilot would arrive shortly.

At the height of Fijian summer, it is absolutely roasting. We were stuffed in that little plane alongside a tropical fruit medley with no air-conditioning. "My God! Where is that pilot?" I muttered with a spot of annoyance creeping into my voice. We could hardly breathe. My happy honeymoon demeanor was starting to wane. Breathe slowly and deeply, Leanne. Relax. This is a magnificent honeymoon adventure, I said silently as rivers of sweat cascaded down my face, arms, and legs. Murray dabbed his head with a handkerchief and smiled at me kindly.

Finally, we saw someone approaching in the distance and assumed it was the pilot. He was strolling lackadaisically toward us, pulling another cart with a small crate on it. In true Fijian style, he was in no hurry. When he arrived, he popped his head inside the piping hot plane and greeted us with a cheery "Bula."

"Thanks for your patience. I just need to load this final box, and then we will be off," he said with a huge grin. "We need to make sure you have all you need out there for your stay. You are the first guests back to the island." His gold tooth caught the sun's heavy rays and glinted at me. My normally rock-solid stomach turned. There was no way he could fit the extra crate into this plane, of that I was quite sure.

I was trying insanely hard to keep from saying something snarky to him. After all, this was our honeymoon. But by God, we were at boiling point. As the streams of sweat ran down my spine, I realized (not for the first time) that patience was not one of my strong suits. I harrumphed again. Murray gently laid his hand on my leg and smartly did not say a thing. The pilot did a little rearranging of the already overstuffed plane and then somehow managed to wondrously wedge his crate into a little spot right near the tail.

As he walked around to his seat, there was an almighty, heart-stopping CRASH, and we were hurled out of our seats, hitting our heads on the plane's ceiling as the plane tipped backward! The weight of all the stuff jammed into the back had forced the plane's tail down, and it had smashed onto the tarmac. And now, the plane's nose pointed skyward. We were jolted backward into a supine position, with our legs reaching straight up toward the sky. A vociferous scream escaped my mouth, "What the hell just happened?" Murray lay there upside down beside me, quietly, gently holding my hand, seemingly unfazed. At that moment I realized I may just have married the calmest person on Earth.

"I think our load may be a tad too heavy," said the way-too chipper pilot with a guffaw. "Hold on tight," he said as he yanked a box out from behind us. In an instant, the plane catapulted back to the upright position with a thundering crack, banging our heads on the hot ceiling again and shooting us back into our sitting position. I screamed again. Murray smiled.

"I guess we should leave that box behind," our bouncy pilot muttered with a chuckle.

What the hell was wrong with these two excruciatingly calm men? We had just about taken off over the ocean in a plane that was so overloaded it could not even stay level just sitting on the tarmac. I was now in a cold sweat, despite the sweltering heat. My heart thundered.

Then I noticed something even more disturbing than the tipped over plane. When the plane had shot back to its normal position, the impact had broken one of the back windows and it now sported a massive crack running its full length from top to bottom. I grunted something to the two unruffled men and pointed to the crack with a quivering finger.

"I think you should get out," said the pilot, his tooth glinting yet again. "We will need to get that window fixed. Why don't you two head on back across the tarmac to that storage shed over there, where you can wait until we get it fixed. I will come and get you when we are ready to depart."

Three hours later, after languishing in a corrugated iron shed full of tropical fruit and veggies, our chirpy pilot returned to us. "We are ready for takeoff in a few minutes. Hurry along now," he said with a smile. He was kidding on the hurry thing, right? We had just waited for hours in temperatures I suspected were found only in Hades, and he had said hurry. I glared at him as we scuttled over to the plane. To my intense horror, I noticed that the cracked window had not been replaced. Instead, an aluminum strip had been riveted over the crack. This was "Fijian fixed." I shuddered.

"Hurry up now," he said as I stood motionless, gawking at our ride to paradise. At that moment, I was wondering which "paradise" I would end up in.

"Nothing to worry about," he chimed when he saw my dismay. "Totally safe. We'll have you on that island in no time."

"Is there no other option than on this plane?" I squeaked. "Boat perhaps?"

"Nope, this is it today." He beamed.

"It may be a week or two until we can get another window for this baby. Most of the planes were evacuated for the storm, so this is it for the day. If you want to get to your resort, then hop right on in, miss."

I gulped and looked up into Murray's steady green eyes. Calmly, he nodded, grabbed my hand, and helped me back into the plane.

"It'll be okay," he said. "Just think of the tales we will be able to tell our kids one day!"

He was right. Twenty minutes later, we were bumping along the little grass runway on Mana Island. I could finally breathe, open my eyes, and release my death grip on Murray's hand. We had made it to the right paradise for a week of wonderment.

• • •

Murray planned to continue some studies at the University of Ottawa. We packed up his little truck and drove across Canada from Saskatoon to Ottawa. We knew no one there, and I had no job opportunities just yet. I could not work in Canada as a physiotherapist until I passed provincial licensing exams. The exams were a requisite to work in any of Canada's ten provinces. Our plan was to both get any job we could find while I studied for my exams and Murray continued his university studies. But we quickly found the job market to be very tough, and jobs were not as easy to come by as we had anticipated.

I was anxious and fearful. I worried about how we would get living accommodations without an income or how we would survive in the first place. Murray's tuition fees were due, and we did not have enough money in the bank to cover them. My panic meter skyrocketed. Despair crept in. We were at the end of our resources. We did not know what to do.

Then a miracle happened. I met a nurse who worked at the National Defense Hospital in Ottawa. She told me she knew of a job opening for a physiotherapist there. She was friends with the physiotherapy department head at the hospital and offered to talk to her on my behalf about the open position. Thanking her, I explained that Canada didn't recognize my New Zealand qualifications. I would have to pass the provincial exams before I could work in my profession, and that could take some time. Nonetheless, she jotted down my phone number and said she would see what she could find out for me.

You can imagine my surprise when the physiotherapy department head called me the following day. The only exception to the provincial licensing requirements in all of Canada was at the National Defense Hospital in Ottawa. As a federal facility, it was not subject to provincial requirements. My New Zealand degree was acceptable for employment at only this one hospital in the entire country. I could hardly believe my ears. I was invited in for an interview, and I began my new job by the end of that week. I marveled once again. Something so much bigger than me was surely working on my behalf.

I don't believe this miracle was just good luck. That job was meant for me. It took a great deal of courage to make that move to Ottawa, not knowing what the future would hold. There were many scary days when we were just coins away from being broke. We took "that one next step" that was in front of us and believed the following step would be apparent. Fantastically, it was.

The funny thing is, even though I have experienced a lifetime of miraculous provisions, I still get very afraid and stressed during difficulties. My mind is a master at fear-mongering tactics and easily finds its way to the worst-case scenario. This is especially so when an immediate solution to a problem is not apparent. Instead of remaining calm and believing that all will work out, my default response is panic. I scramble around trying to force change. I am sure you know what this feels like, since it is an all too common response.

When I find I am heading down this fearful thought path, I now know how to halt the trip.

How?

I consciously recall all the miracles, big and small, that have happened to me. I remind myself that the *power of things unseen* that worked for me all those years ago in Dublin and Canada are still working for me today, no matter how fraught my current situation might appear. I choose to believe that I have all that I need for each moment in time. And in reality, I do.

CHAPTER 5

· · · · · · · · · · · · · · · · · ·

Sit Back and Relax

The first couple of years as newlyweds in Canada were magical. Our first Christmas together, Murray gave me my inaugural pair of ice skates. He told me that I could not live in Canada without owning a pair of skates. True. It was a freezing -25°C that day, and I was a little hesitant since I had never ice skated. We bundled up from head to toe and headed to the Rideau Canal Skateway. It is the longest skating rink in the world, spanning almost eight kilometers long. "Piece of cake," my boyish-sounding husband assured me. Easy for him to say since he played hockey and had been on ice skates most of his life. I laced up my sparkly new skates and somehow wobbled to my feet. Murray then gave me a skating 101 crash course. This included directions on how to stay upright and how to stop, which might entail running into a barrier if necessary. That sounded feasible, if not likely. He then grasped my mitted hand, and we took off. We skated the entire sixteen kilometers there and back in the crispy, icy cold of that festive day. I felt like I was flying. I did not fall once, thanks to my strong husband pulling me along each time I teetered. I was ecstatic. We arrived back at one of the concession huts set out on the ice and finished off the day with a cup of piping hot apple cider and a warm BeaverTails pastry. The whole day was enchanting. It was a Christmas I would not forget.

Within just a couple of years of getting married, we were expecting our first child and decided to move back to New Zealand so I could be near my family. Murray loved New Zealand and was keen to live there awhile.

Our trip back to my old home involved another flight to remember.

We had several stopovers and plane changes from Ottawa to Auckland. The flight into Los Angeles International Airport was terribly delayed, so we were sure we would miss our connection to Auckland. We were booked on the last flight to NZ that day, but because of our delay, we were convinced we would have to spend the night in LA. While we pondered what to do about this unwelcome development, the captain announced over the crackling sound system that we were venturing into bad weather. It was time to buckle up. Within seconds, the heavens opened. We saw forked lightning outside the windows as our plane was buffeted by heavy rain and winds. We were mercilessly tossed around by the power of the elements. It really was one of those white-knuckle type of flights, lurching up and down, backward and forward. More than a few of those nasty little paper bags were in use up and down the aisles. Eww! Now my stomach was churning too. I was turning a deep shade of green.

Relief flooded through my tense body with the pilot's announcement that we would be landing momentarily. I noticed I had Murray's hand in a viselike grip. He would probably be relieved to get circulation back in his pinkies, but of course he just smiled sweetly at me and didn't even try to wiggle free.

It is challenging for me to describe what happened next, because it all happened so quickly. We heard the landing gear whir out of the wheel wells and were mere feet from hitting the runway. I braced myself for a jolt on touchdown. Suddenly, the engines roared at full throttle, the nose snapped up toward the sky, and we rocketed heavenward. As we were shooting ever higher, we heard a viciously loud crack and our plane gave a horrific shudder. Passengers gasped, babies howled, and old ladies fainted.

A few moments later, our jovial British pilot came over the intercom and in perfect Queen's English said, "Sorry about that, folks. We were cleared for landing, but just prior to touchdown, we saw another plane on the runway. The bang you heard during our ascent was a slight electrical discharge as our aircraft was struck by lightning. We will have you on the ground in a few minutes. So sit back and relax while we wait to be cleared for landing again."

Was he freaking kidding? Sit back and relax? I was seven and a half months pregnant, we had just about crashed into another plane, and then our plane had been struck by lightning!

"Shh," said my amazingly chill husband. "It's okay." Baby hormones and adrenaline were swirling within me, and I wanted to shriek and wail. But I knew he was right. Poltergeistlike behavior would not make the moment any better, so I sat quietly and concentrated on peaceful breathing.

As we neared the landing strip for a second attempt, you could have heard a pin drop in the cabin. There was total silence as all two hundred passengers waited for touchdown.

Thud! Bounce. Our tires hit the ground, and the sound of roaring brakes pulling us to an abrupt stop was quite simply the stuff of my most beautiful dreams. Suddenly, every passenger broke into loud applause and cheering. It felt great to be on terra firma.

We ran as fast as a seven-and-a-half-month-pregnant lady's legs would carry her to our next flight. Thankfully, it had been delayed. We arrived just before the doors closed and boarded our 747 heading for Auckland. Unfortunately, the only two seats left were in the very last row. They would not recline. We had a stopover in Honolulu, after which we had to reboard. I started to whimper like a baby. "I can't possibly go another seven hours sitting upright," I blubbered to Murray. "I am not getting back on that aircraft." I dug my feet into the carpet and stood like a statue. Cajoling an emotional, exhausted, pregnant woman with terrible heartburn, a sore back, and extremely puffy feet is no easy task, but my imperturbable, long-suffering husband succeeded at the task and finally got me back onto the plane. Despite my sniveling, I realized how good it was to be returning to my homeland with my kind husband for the birth of our first child.

At the end of December, we welcomed our beautiful Victoria into the world.

Ahhhh . . . the miracle of new life. It was truly fantastic to hold my precious, tiny baby in my arms. As her mother, I had the amazing privilege of nurturing her. It was my job to help her grow to her full potential. The magnitude of love that I felt for my child was indescribable. She was perfect in every way.

Soon after Victoria joined our world, we purchased our own little two-bedroom home just minutes from the ocean. We loved spending our spare time hiking, beach walking, swimming, and exploring the beauty all around us. Murray had found a wonderful job working in the computer field, and I worked part time as a physiotherapist. We settled comfortably into suburbia.

More joy arrived in our lives two years later when I gave birth to our second daughter, Julia. From the moment she arrived, she had things to do and places to go. I was besotted with her, just as I was with Victoria. We loved the fact that our girls had such different personalities.

All the while, something new was awakening within us. We just couldn't see ourselves living in suburbia forever, no matter how good it was. We were yearning to do something more with our lives. I had such a keen sense that I had been given so much in life and that I wanted to be able to give back. Murray felt the same. We couldn't silence this. We knew it deep within.

When Julia was just six weeks old, we started making moves. We received a letter from my close friends in Dublin. They were still running the program I had been involved in while living there. The letter told us about available opportunities with the nonprofit throughout Europe. As we read it, something clicked for us both. We knew it was time to move back to Europe.

"I think that is a terrible mistake!" my dear father said to me when I shared our decision with him and Mum. I was a little taken aback. My parents had always been super supportive. They epitomized parents who raised their children to be independent individuals, able to make their own decisions. Dad had a plethora of sensible reasons why packing up and leaving our comfortable and secure lifestyle, with two little ones, was a disastrous decision. Yet we just couldn't rid ourselves of the fact that we believed this was what we needed to do. When we looked at it logically, I had to agree with my father. He had a lot of really good points. What we planned to do was outright folly. We had a six-week-old baby and a two-year-old toddler. We had zero savings, no paying jobs awaiting us, and a house to sell in a down market. It just made no sense. It was nuts.

Nonetheless, after several phone calls and letters to confirm our appointments, we were hired to head up a training program for youth in Liverpool, and we had to be on the job in six weeks. Once we put things into motion, several small miracles occurred.

We put our house up for sale and it sold quickly, despite the negative utterings of our real estate agent. He had told us that we'd lose money on our home, but we didn't.

Murray had a British passport, so living in the UK was no problem for him. The girls were on his passport, so they were covered as well. I, however, needed a permanent residency visa to reside in the UK. As the wife of a British citizen, I was entitled to this visa. So as soon as we decided to move, we submitted the necessary paperwork to the British Embassy. Unfortunately it was a process that took time, more time than we realized.

We moved out of our house, finished our jobs, and packed up our few belongings. We regularly phoned the embassy and got the typically annoying recording about how processing times were abnormally slow. Don't you just love that message? It sure as hell made me want to choke somebody.

We spent the last few days with my parents in their home. Everything was ready, but the British Embassy hadn't returned my passport with the precious visa stamp. I could not travel without it. We had purchased nonrefundable tickets and were due to fly out the following evening. Still nothing.

The night before we left, we packed our suitcases and enjoyed our final family dinner. It was kind of weird because everyone knew that I did not have my passport. My parents still thought we were a little crazy, but they were kindly going along with our harebrained plan and giving us a send-off.

The following morning, I headed down the long driveway at my parents' home and sat on the fence waiting for the mailman to arrive. He pulled up and handed me the mail. There, on the top, sat a package from the British Embassy with my stamped passport tucked away safely inside. I ran back to the house whooping and hollering. We had the "all clear" to leave in just a couple of hours. Our faith had been tested once again, but we had confirmation that what we were doing was right, even though it was crazy and far from normal.

CHAPTER 6

· · · · · · · · · · · · · · · · · ·

A Jammy Piece and an Overhead Contraption

It is one thing to take off around the world to enjoy a new adventure when you are on your own, but a totally different scenario when you have a new baby and toddler in tow. It was daunting. Yet here we were, moving to England, because we were convinced it was the right path for us.

We finally arrived in Liverpool a couple of days later and surveyed the studio apartment the nonprofit had provided us. The place was unbelievably tiny. How were the four of us going to live in a single room?

The next day, we checked our bank account and saw that the money from the sale of our house had not lasted as long as we had expected.

I felt sick to my stomach. We had just twelve pounds left to our names. Everything suddenly seemed so much more difficult than I had anticipated. Once the girls were asleep for the night, I collapsed onto our small bed and wept. What in the hell had we done by moving across the world with two babies and next to nothing? Fear came tumbling in, and I couldn't shake my anxiety. It was a very dark night for me because I was so scared. No matter how hard I tried to tell myself that everything would work out for us, I could not shut off my tears.

The nonprofit we worked with did not have a traditional financial model. Every one of its ten thousand employees around the globe was a volunteer. This model worked fine if you were only involved in a short-term project, but it was much more difficult for long-term employees. Each person was 100 percent responsible to fundraise his or her own income. Typically, they raised money from family, friends, church groups, or from savings and investments.

Prior to leaving New Zealand, we had managed to fundraise just enough to cover our anticipated monthly expenses, with nothing to spare. We knew we'd be living on a shoestring budget, but this hadn't deterred us. Once we arrived in the UK and the reality of our financial limitations hit, doubt began to creep in. Fear that we would not have the means to provide for our kids' needs swirled through my brain. I found our living situation extremely stressful.

Although our work was rewarding, the next couple of years turned out to be unquestionably difficult. This was mainly because we lived on meager resources in an excruciatingly small space with rambunctious children in a low-socioeconomic inner-city environment.

We worked in an area with an extremely high number of single-parent families, and I often wondered how these parents managed to get through each day without a wonderful partner, like Murray, with whom to share the load. Looking at those around me helped change my perspective. I realized that I was a genuinely lucky person. I found strength to be happy and thankful even when day-to-day living was not always easy. My perspective slowly shifted. I realized that real happiness is not dependent on circumstance. It comes from within, from having a positive attitude, and from being grateful for all the blessings that surround us.

· · ·

When the girls were two and four years old, we moved to Scotland. The nonprofit had an urgent need for an information technology professional to run the tech department, and it seemed like a perfect fit for Murray. The job was in Paisley, another fairly tough town, just outside of Glasgow. It was still a volunteer position, and the responsibility to fundraise our own income continued. We were struggling to make ends meet, so we needed to look at other ways to supplement our income.

Murray secured a part-time computer programming job. I secured a part-time job as a physiotherapist at a local hospital. At first, I could barely understand what everyone was saying. The Glaswegian accent was close to unintelligible! I became adept at just nodding and saying "ah ha" during most conversations.

After living in a tiny studio apartment, I desperately wanted to get a "real home" again. We thought that our two part-time jobs, in addition to the income from our fundraising efforts, might provide enough income for us to buy a home. When the bank approved us to purchase an entry-level property with no down payment, I could hardly believe it. It was thrilling, like birds singing at sunrise. I twirled out of the bank with deep gratitude in my heart and a skip in my step that had been missing for a while. We found a small ground-floor, sandstone tenement flat very close to the downtown area where we worked. Since we did not own a car, the location was ideal.

We were unquestionably fit. We walked for miles every day, depositing the girls at their schools and then continuing on to our jobs. The reverse trips were made later in the day. My lanky six-foot-four husband has a fairly quick stride. While I took Victoria to her school in one direction, he took two-year-old Julia to her preschool in the opposite direction. It was almost comical to watch the two of them walking along. Murray was in brisk full stride with Julia running just to keep up with him for the entire one-mile trip. We often joke that this contributed to her great success as a cross-country runner in high school.

Our new flat needed much love and upgrading, but it didn't matter because it was our home. Thank God it had more space too. While it was not in the most salubrious part of town, it was ours.

We shared a backyard with five other tenement flats, and it often felt like we lived in a British TV series. This lifestyle was so vastly different from the one I had grown up in. Mothers would call out of the windows of their top-floor flats to ask their kids whether they wanted a "jammy piece." If they did, a jam sandwich would come flying past my ground-floor window to the child playing in the garden below. It was lunchtime!

• • •

The Scots are such wonderfully warm, kind, and funny people. Gordon was no exception. He was unemployed, single, very handy, and had plenty of time on his hands. He offered to help us with renovating our flat in return for meals and a place to hang out. I thought it to be a great trade. I love to cook, and my New Zealand roots make me very hospitable. There were always people at our home, sharing in our family and our meals. So one more would make no difference.

Gradually, we tore the interior of the flat apart and started to rebuild. In some rooms, we removed more than fifteen layers of wallpaper to discover the original hand-painted poppy pattern from the 1800s. When we pulled off the baseboard in the living room, we found newspaper from the 1870s stuffed in behind it as insulation. It was a fascinating read.

I came home from work one afternoon to find Gordon in a haze of dust and rubble. He had just ripped the kitchen apart. Big chunks of a concrete mantel from the old kitchen fireplace lay in our entry hallway. It was our biggest renovation project thus far. The original kitchen had nothing more than a fireplace, a sink, and a cupboard. There was also an awesome clothes-drying rack hanging from the ceiling. We hoisted it up and down on a pulley system. We did not have a clothes dryer, so I loved this contraption. I just had to remember that when guests arrived for dinner, my underwear should not be hanging above their heads.

That evening, while I was stripping the kitchen wallpaper, I developed a horrible headache and I could not shake it. I finally abandoned my task, ran a hot bath (there was no shower in the flat yet), and started to soak. I hoped relaxing in the tub would ease the pain. By the time I got out of it, my head was really pounding. Painkillers weren't working, so I put myself to bed just after eight p.m., leaving Murray and Gordon to continue with the kitchen demolition.

By one a.m., I was in agony and screaming from pain. Murray called the emergency doctor, and within minutes, the doctor called for an ambulance to take me directly to the emergency room. He suspected that I had meningitis.

The doctor was correct. I remained in the hospital for days. Poor Murray was left to look after the girls, work two jobs, and live in a home reduced to an empty shell filled with detritus. Thankfully, we had a great network of really wonderful friends at the nonprofit. They dropped off meals and took turns with childcare while Murray was at work. Gordon was a rock star and worked day and night on the renovations. Nevertheless, it was in times like this, when nothing was going as I would have expected, that I really missed an easy, comfortable environment with my family around me for support. This was when I would catch myself asking, "Why am I doing this?"

But I knew the answer: I was doing what I was meant to be doing.

. . .

On occasion, people have questioned our decision to take our young daughters to live in far from perfect conditions. I understand their concern. I like to point out, however, that no matter what our living conditions were, our daughters have always had an incredibly loving, caring, and safe home. From a young age they learned to be real. We never hid anything from them. They saw our victories and our struggles. When we faced adversity, they saw us find a way through it. We showed them how to be grateful and find the best in every situation. We taught them how to give, how to have faith, how to work hard, and how to love.

Our girls received a richness of life experiences that most children do not enjoy. We always provided them with all that they needed and more. I soon realized that what was right for Murray and I was also perfect for our daughters, even though our lifestyle ran counter to "normal."

I must add that I now look at my two incredible adult daughters with awe and pride. They are undeniably amazing human beings and have thrived, even with the "far from normal" upbringing they had.

CHAPTER 7

....

The Elevator Shaft and a Love Affair

Life is a journey, brimming with exciting choices along the way. Frequently, Murray and I chose a very spontaneous route for our lives, one that many people would shy away from. We listened to our *inner voice* and made decisions based on the whispers we heard inside of us. We moved forward into the unknown, often without the ability to see more than one step in front of us. It meant that sometimes life appeared to be scary and full of challenges to overcome. Despite this, we were rarely disappointed. In fact, it was tremendous to see the adventure and purpose that each step finally led us to.

Living in the UK was an example of this. It was a stepping stone for the next fascinating and fulfilling season we were about to enter. Our years in Liverpool and then Paisley, living in less than perfect conditions, played an integral role in the preparation for what was ahead. We were stretched way outside of our comfort level. We learned to find pleasure in small things and to be grateful for our many blessings. It was a time of tremendous growth. I seriously doubt we would have learned those things had we remained in New Zealand or Canada.

I find it curious that life journeys are seldom straightforward. In fact, they tend to be quite circuitous. That is what makes them so much fun. So often we take a step that leads to another step that we could never have envisioned, and so on. Now, a new door we could never have imagined was about to open—one we would never have found had we not lived in Scotland.

The early nineties was a period of truly momentous change in Europe. By the end of 1989, Communist regimes were toppling across Europe. A full-blown revolution arose in Poland and spread to Hungary, East Germany, Bulgaria, Czechoslovakia, and eventually Romania. In November 1989, we watched live TV from Berlin and were stunned as we saw thousands of Germans scale and break down the Berlin Wall. This wall was indisputably the most visible symbol of Communism in Europe. After decades of oppression, Eastern Europe was finally opening its doors and welcoming democracy.

Romania was the country that most interested me. The Romanian Revolution started in the city of Timișoara and spread rapidly throughout the country. It culminated in the show trial and execution of longtime Communist leader Nicolae Ceaușescu, bringing to an end more than forty years of cruel Communist rule. It was the only Warsaw Pact country that had endured a violent revolution and executed its leader.

News stories depicting events in Romania over the past four decades captivated me. It was heart-wrenching to hear detailed descriptions of what people had endured because of their leader's greed and depravity. Stories of inhumane and barbaric state-run orphanages surfaced. On several occasions, I could not stop crying because I was so deeply affected by what I saw and heard on TV. Something about Romania captured my attention in a huge way. I couldn't get it out of my head. One day, while I was watching a documentary about recent events there, something spoke to me loudly and clearly. Deep within me, I knew I would be a part of the change that was coming to this country. I just knew it without a doubt.

Shortly afterward, I heard of an opportunity to join a short-term medical team going to a village in Romania. Immediately, I signed up to volunteer for the two-week trip. Murray offered to stay home with the girls while I set out on a journey that would change our lives forever.

• • •

One of my first memories of arriving in Romania was the complete and utter chaos that greeted us as we entered Bucharest's Otopeni Airport. The airport, like many places in the city, was still undergoing construction that had begun many years earlier.

Suitcases were piled in great heaps among mounds of debris. Happy travelers were expected to rummage through these heaps to find their luggage. Guards with semiautomatic rifles patrolled the chaos. People clamored to get through security checkpoints.

We learned early on that bribing was a way of life. I had arrived with my very Western ideals and thought bribing was a terrible thing. Then a lovely Romanian friend explained that on some occasions it was really just like tipping in the USA. Service workers earned so little that it helped to supplement their income. Okay, I could understand that. All the same, it still took me some time before I could work out when to and when not to "tip," because sometimes it really was just straight-out extortion. This was a very different culture, and I clearly had a lot to learn.

My first experience in paying a bribe occurred within minutes of my arrival into Romania. In a flash, I realized that I would not get through customs until I produced American dollars, which I duly did. The gate opened, and I hustled through the crowd to meet up with the rest of the members of my group, who had all handed over their valuable dollars as well.

Before we made the seven-hour drive to the small town in Transylvania where we would stay, our Romanian contact, Dorin, who met us at the airport, took us sightseeing in Bucharest. We headed to Palatul Parlamentului (the Palace of the Parliament), located in central Bucharest. It was beyond impressive. I gaped at its monstrous size. Composed of twenty-three parts, it is the third most massive building in the world and holds the world record for being the heaviest building. It was truly a spectacular sight.

Dorin, my new friend, needed to meet someone at one of the office buildings nearby in the Dealul Arsenalului district. For some reason, he invited me to join him. I love meeting new people, so I jumped at his invitation. I find meeting the local people in cultures new to me infinitely more interesting than just sightseeing. Bucharest was no exception.

Dorin and I parted from the rest of our group to find his friend. As we peeled off, I quickly realized nothing in the area was numbered or even remotely organized. After a good hour of searching, we arrived at what he suspected was the correct building. We entered the lobby, and I distinctly remember thinking how deserted it looked. I mentioned this to Dorin, who told me that lots of buildings were only partially completed and that he wasn't completely sure that we had located the right place. He thought that the office we were looking for was located on the top floor, so we decided to use the elevator. He punched the button, and we heard it grind into action and slowly lumber down to us.

We got into the decrepit-looking elevator, which slowly jerked its way up to the top floor. When we finally arrived—by golly it really was the slowest elevator I had ever been in—the doors slowly juddered apart, giving the impression that they were just too tired to function for a minute longer. We stepped over the threshold and out into what appeared to be a partially constructed and totally vacant set of offices. My "deserted building" hunch had indeed been correct. Clearly we had the wrong place. We hopped back into the elevator to return to the ground floor and continue the search for Dorin's friend. During our descent, the fun began. The elevator lurched violently, and we heard a terrible grinding noise. All went deathly silent. Our elevator had come to a halt in between floors. I felt sick.

Dorin calmly smiled at me. "No problem," he said when he saw the look on my face. He gently pushed the buttons, one after another, while I waited for the elevator to lurch back into action. Nothing. Feeling a little alarmed, I picked up the emergency phone. Dead. I punched the emergency button, to which Dorin knowingly shook his head and said, "No. It will not work." After a few minutes of banging on the doors, yelling for help, mashing buttons, and jumping up and down like a crazy woman while Dorin stood annoyingly still with a smile on his face, I realized that we needed to take some other kind of action. It was pretty obvious that no help would be coming our way any time soon.

By now I had realized Dorin had an extremely calm demeanor. The thought ran through my addled mind, that I had an uncanny way of surrounding myself with ridiculously calm men. Dorin serenely looked at me and said, "We need to find a way out of here."

"Ha! That is the understatement of all understatements!" I wanted to yell, but instead I just swallowed hard. I was not feeling very gracious and was desperately trying to hold my tongue and reign in my panic. I just could not believe he was so calm. He was so matter of fact that he might as well have been talking about the weather with me over a cup of coffee. Here we were stuck between floors in an elevator, in an abandoned building with no help in sight, and he was taking it all in stride. I tried to gather my nerves as best I could.

"Right," I croaked. "Any suggestions?" My lack of pleasure at being trapped in small, dark places meant that the terror inside of me had begun to rise rather sharply, despite my efforts to appear cool.

"Let's see if we can get the doors open," was Dorin's very practical response.

Of course. But that suggestion was easier said than done. For the next ten minutes, using all our strength, we attempted to pry open the securely closed internal elevator doors. Finally, they opened a crack and we peered into the lift shaft and saw a second set of doors to the floor several feet above us. My already raspy breathing became a whole lot shallower as I grasped the severity of our situation. I shuddered but pretended to be brave so Dorin wouldn't think his new friend was a total wuss.

Once we opened the interior doors a bit more, Dorin said in his wonderfully tranquil voice, "Well now, I think we should climb up to those exterior doors and try to pull them apart."

"Rightio! You first!" I squeaked. Yikes! This was getting ridiculous. We had to climb into an elevator shaft.

Off he went through these doors like a ninja, hoisting himself upward toward the closed doors above. He sort of balanced on the top of our elevator car and started to bang and yank on the second set of doors. They suddenly shot wide open, and I could see several ankles and feet in front of them. The sweet sound of cheering and clapping filled my ears. There were people on this floor, and they were applauding merrily. Before I knew what was happening, big meaty hands reached down to pull me up through the elevator shaft and to the floor above.

Within a blink, I was whisked out of the elevator and lying on my belly, splayed on the ground in a fairly unladylike manner. I looked up at my rescuers, noticing that not one person acted like this was even the slightest bit odd. They pulled me up to a standing position and dusted me off. They were all gabbing away in Romanian, so I just stood there nodding and smiling. Relief surged through me in quite a lovely way. Much chatter ensued between Dorin and our rescuers as I looked at them questioningly. Finally, after about ten minutes, Dorin explained that they were insisting we should not have used the elevator because it wasn't working properly.

Really? Had no one thought to put up an "Out of Order" sign? I wanted to shriek. Dorin patiently explained to me that they were used to things not working, and these types of hazards were just part and parcel of everyday life in Romania.

I clearly had a lot to learn.

By now, I was over my yearning to meet new people. Suddenly, sightseeing seemed like a grand idea. I breathed an audible sigh of relief when Dorin suggested we abandon the search for his friend. It was time to join up with our group and head out of Bucharest. I reckoned I had endured enough adrenaline highs for the day. I was happy to be leaving this place.

• • •

I love to remember my first impressions of new countries and cultures. There is something about the smells and sounds that stick with me. I love that I can still smell a place in my mind, even though it has been years since I was there.

That first day in Romania is still lodged in my senses: It was February, so it was genuinely cold. There was slushy snow everywhere, and everything smelled appropriately damp. Our team of ten piled into what felt like an excruciatingly small minivan, along with our luggage and some supplies Dorin had picked up in Bucharest. We didn't have an inch of wiggle room. None! I was sitting crouched in the back on top of luggage. My head was hitting the ceiling of the van. The heating didn't work, and we had a seven-hour overnight drive to Aiud. I was absolutely exhausted by this time, but I was so cold, numb, and bent over that there was no way I could even nod off for a few moments of shuteye. I think the word "miserable" probably best describes the way I felt on that journey.

There were no hotels in the town, so we were hosted in the homes of local residents. Those early post-Communist days made me feel as though I had stepped back into what I imagined the 1940s were like. It was like time had stood still after World War II. Homes were small and quite basic. The water supply was frequently cut off throughout the day, and in many homes there was no hot water at all. Power was hit or miss. Only a few people had telephones, and those who did shared party lines with several neighbors.

I saw people living in shacks with big holes in the walls. There were many beggars living on the streets. There was abject poverty everywhere one looked.

Only the very privileged owned cars. There was only one model: a Romanian-made Dacia. Many of those cars were broken down because parts were seldom available or repairs unaffordable. It was common to see horses and carts being used for transportation. It was hard for me to fathom that this was Europe in the 1990s.

Our kind and gracious hosts gave us their nicest rooms and cooked us delicious meals from their incredibly meager supplies. That's how Romanians roll. At the time, I didn't realize how sacrificial their hospitality really was. They would go without, so that they could give to us. These kind people had learned to survive the harsh Communist regime by helping one another.

I instantly fell in love with our hostess, Fibia. She had a beautiful spirit. She was a very smart woman in her fifties who spoke some English, and I loved nothing more than sitting and chatting with her. I wanted to find out all that I could about her. It amazed me when she said she felt that she was old. By the time a person reached their fifties in Romania, many felt that their life was pretty much over. Decades of hardship and oppressive rule had taken their toll on the human spirit and on the body.

It reminded me just how lucky I was to grow up in New Zealand. I had not lived with great oppression and hardship. My grandfather, then in his late nineties, was still alive. He continued to drive a car, walked a couple of miles a day, and was as sharp as a tack. He didn't feel terribly old at all. He was almost twice Fibia's age and yet seemed about the same age.

I shared a bed with Becky, a delightful Scottish doctor, who instantly became a good friend. There is nothing like sharing a small bed with a stranger for several days to make you become bosom buddies. Thank goodness she was a genuinely lovely person with a great sense of humor to boot. There were a lot of times on that trip when we quickly realized it was best just to laugh.

While in Romania, we distributed aid and helped with the medical needs of the community. In the back of my mind, I continuously assessed the variety of needs and tried to figure out how we could partner with this community in a more long-term capacity. We had so much in the West, and I wanted to find a way to bring help to this nation that was still reeling from decades of cruelty and deprivation. I wanted to be a part of something larger, not just a two-week trip to distribute aid and give medical help.

One day, Becky and I paid a visit to a sick older woman, the wife of a well-known Hungarian artist living in the town. She was bedridden. The pungent odor of illness lingered in the closed, shuttered room. As Becky examined her and questioned her on the treatments she received, we discovered that she was far from elderly. However, she suffered from heart disease and was unable to get basic medicine. She would be fully functional if she had access to the medication she needed. We found this was not an uncommon occurrence: The unavailability of basic medicines was great. As we worked our way through the community visiting the sick, we compiled a list of much needed medications we planned to source and bring back to those in need.

By the end of my two-week stay in Aiud, I knew I would come back here. In a very short time, I had developed a deep friendship with Dorin. He clearly had knowledge of the need in his community and a steadfast drive to bring change. Becky was certain she would be back as well. Together, we began to make plans for our future work in Romania. I arrived home from that trip having left a little part of myself there. It's hard to describe how in just two weeks I was smitten with such a deep love for this nation. But I was.

I knew I would return soon . . .

CHAPTER 8

· · · · · · · · · · · · · · · · ·

Stinging Cheeks and Gratitude

I was like a dog with a bone. I could not stop thinking about Romania, and of course, because I am such a chatterbox, I couldn't stop talking about it either. Murray listened to everything I told him and processed it in his own quiet way. He was amazed by how much I could talk on this one subject. I just couldn't help it. I was truly smitten.

There were projects galore in which we could get involved. The early post-revolution days were still a time for relief. Development would follow. One thing I could do was spread awareness of the great need. So I did. I sent out letters and visited schools, churches, youth groups, medical facilities, and local pubs. I was relentless. I started a fundraising campaign. I found that Scots are extremely generous and big-hearted. Before long we had resources pouring in to help. In addition to financial aid, we had medical supplies, drugs, clothes, food, household items, and toys streaming in. We needed medicine more than anything else. Becky compiled a list of medical supplies that would have the greatest impact and were unavailable in the town. She obtained some drugs from medical supply companies, and others we purchased. We worked together on a strategy to bring aid to the village of Aiud.

After incessant discussion, Murray and I decided it was time to visit Romania. We would go during the summer and take the girls. We needed a large vehicle to transport all the donations we had gathered. Murray would transport our stockpile of supplies by road, and the girls and I would fly. We would converge in Aiud. Our friend Gordon had a large blue van. Unknowingly, my continuous chatter about Romania while we worked together on our ongoing flat renovations had infected him. Before long he offered his van to transport the ginormous, heaving mountain of supplies piled on our living room floor.

Murray and Gordon set out on the five-day drive from Scotland to Romania. The van was groaning from the sheer quantity of goods squeezed into it. I marveled at my husband's superhuman packing abilities. The trip took them through England, Belgium, Germany, Austria, and Hungary. It was an 1,800-mile journey that we, as a family, would get very used to making over the next several years.

Victoria and Julia were not yet three and five. They were extremely fair-skinned little girls—Murray was their father after all!—and the cutest things you'd ever lay eyes on. Victoria had long, thick strawberry-blond hair, and Julia had a mass of very white, fluffy curls that framed her little head like a halo. They were altogether pretty darn adorable. When we arrived in Bucharest, there was no denying that they were foreign.

Romanians generally have an olive complexion and they found my pale-skinned girls to be a total novelty. "Angels" was a word I often heard used to describe them. Complete strangers regularly just walked up and touched Victoria and Julia while uttering an endearing string of words that none of us understood.

The local women had this unusual custom of pinching little kids' cheeks as a show of affection. Personally, I have never worked out how pinching anything is affectionate, but what do I know. Unfortunately, sometimes the pinching was a little too enthusiastic. Naturally, the girls disliked this practice, mainly because it resulted in stinging red cheeks. I endeavored to divert these strangers from their cheek-pinching penchant, but to no avail. My tiny blonde girls were definitely a huge hit, like a new show had just come to town.

I have a lot of great memories from that first summer in Romania. It was a wonderful adventure for the kids. We stayed at Fibia's home. The kitties, puppies, and chickens that were part of her home's rural setting were the hot ticket items for our girls, who were used to living in an inner-city tenement.

Victoria loved nature and kittens. Her days were full of cuddling kittens, collecting wildflowers, eating wild mulberries, and picking vegetables from the garden. She visited the chicken house throughout the day, and her delight at finding eggs and delivering them to Fibia was palpable.

Julia, who was my dog whisperer even at two years old, was besotted with the puppies. She spent hours cuddling them and wrapping them in rags that she managed to purloin from around the yard. One day, she put their ears in "hairstyles" with clothespins that she found lying on the porch. As you'd imagine, this didn't end happily. The puppies started yelping, and then Julia started howling because she was so upset that she had hurt her precious fur babies.

There was a lot of dust and dirt. Grass and paving were rare. Showers were a luxury. Before putting the children to bed at the end of the day, I would endeavor to get my very grubby little urchins into some semblance of cleanliness with a washcloth and a basin of water. One day I looked down at Julia sitting on the porch cuddling a sleeping puppy and saw fleas running up her arms. I just couldn't convince her to leave the puppies alone. Quite frankly it was near impossible to pry a puppy from her arms once she had a hold of it. From then on, I realized I would have to be extremely rigorous with our daily hygiene efforts.

• • •

It was wonderful to distribute aid to those in need. It is extremely humbling to be continuously thanked for such basic things as toothbrushes, soap, vitamins, and aspirin. Seeing poverty with your own eyes alters the way you think. You recognize how you are blessed with so much simply because of where you were born and raised. This experience deeply affected me. My gratitude levels soared on those visits.

I often wonder why gratitude does not always come easily to the human race. All too often, the more we have, the more we complain. What a strange phenomenon. But I see it in myself. To this day, even after all I have experienced, if my life isn't going the way I would like it to, I often complain or have a negative attitude. I don't think I am alone in this.

In our society, we are bombarded from many angles with the notion that life should be picture-book perfect. When things fall short of perfection, as they most often do, it is easy to feel as though our world has fallen apart. Rather than looking at the things we think are missing, we should focus on all the good we have and remain grateful. This is essential to achieving success and happiness.

I saw this time and again in Romania in those early years. People who had suffered tremendous pain found a way to be thankful for what they had. They did not feel sorry for themselves, and believe me, it appeared they certainly could have found a lot to feel sorry about. Instead they looked at their blessings, no matter how meager, and rejoiced in them.

Because we live in a society predisposed to want "easy," it seems absurd to be thankful for our struggles and difficulties. Yet I believe we grow through hardship. Romania was a nation that had been through decades of terrible hardship and everywhere I looked, people were full of hope and gratitude. It was inspiring to meet people who were so grateful amidst their struggles to survive.

CHAPTER 9

· · · · · · · · · · · · · · · · ·

Plum Brandy and a Tummy Bug

O ver the next couple of years, our fundraising efforts continued with gusto. Aid for Romania kept pouring in. We saw a remarkable increase in requests for help from the community in Aiud. Soon, some of our donors asked to join us in our travels. They wanted to see Romania firsthand and volunteer their time and energy. So began a new stage in our Romanian work: organizing volunteer teams that traveled with us to this amazing country.

There was still very limited medical care in Aiud. Dorin told us that a new medical clinic with quality care was of utmost importance in his town, and so this became one of our first big projects. With Dorin and

Dr. Becky (my first-trip bedmate), we started a fundraising campaign. We worked on the plans for a clinic. Before long, we had raised enough funds to buy an existing building that we would transform into this new facility. We put together a summer team of volunteers from different countries with varied skills to work on the renovation project. Medical supplies and equipment for the project continued flooding in.

My mum called me from New Zealand on the day we were due to fly out to Romania with our first volunteer team. She was at the hospital with my dad, who had just suffered a massive heart attack. He was going in for bypass surgery sometime later that day. All I wanted to do was get on a plane directly to Auckland, instead of flying to Romania with Murray and the girls. Despite his condition, Dad got on the phone and unequivocally told me how upset he would be if I canceled my trip and put our summer project on hold. He was emphatic I should not change my plans. I felt so torn. I hung up the phone and sat for a while, thinking it all through. Logic told me to go to New Zealand because of Dad's grave situation. Nonetheless, I could not quell the quiet voice inside me telling me not to worry about Dad. Crazy. Of course I would worry! I found it ironic that I was heading to Romania to work on building a medical clinic and here Dad was on the other side of the world in a world-class medical center about to have open-heart surgery performed by a highly skilled surgeon. This option would not have been available for him in Aiud. Murray and I discussed various scenarios, and I finally made the difficult decision to continue with our trip to Romania. Despite my angst, I also felt tremendous internal peace about my gut decision.

We arrived at Fibia's home after a long day of travel, during which my thoughts and prayers were obviously back in New Zealand with Dad. A big hug from Fibia immediately set me off bawling. I blubbered about Dad's situation and asked if I could use their phone to call home.

"Of course," Fibia said while stroking the tears from my face. She picked up the phone and found that someone else down the road was using the line. She kindly interrupted their conversation and told them it was urgent. She then kept trying to access the operator. Finally, after an excruciatingly long wait, someone at the switchboard picked up. I was so excited to hear Fibia say the words "Noua Zeelanda," followed by Mum's phone number. I reached to grab the phone from Fibia, but she promptly hung up. What?

Gently, she explained that we now had to wait for the operator to get a line to New Zealand. This would take some time. Again, I could not fathom how this was the 1990s and that it was going to take a couple of hours just to place a simple phone call to my family in New Zealand. Despite my frustration, I was also painfully aware of how difficult life was for many in Romania. I could not imagine dealing with this awkward telephone process every day. When I mentioned this to Fibia, she assured me that most people in town did not have a phone. It was a privilege to have one. We were lucky to be able to request a call from the comfort of home. Wow, that offered a different perspective.

While waiting, my emotions had kicked into high gear, perhaps because I was tired from travel. I imagined all the worst-case scenarios in bright technicolor. I let fear seize me. I imagined Dad had died. I did something very silly. I began to second-guess my decision to come to Romania. I was a mess when the phone finally rang several hours later. Mum came on the line and told me Dad had just come out of successful quadruple bypass surgery. He was in the intensive care unit and doing well. Mum and I were sobbing so much that we could hardly speak. I promised to call back the next day if I could get a line.

I fell into bed that night totally exhausted but unable to sleep from the sheer emotion of the day. As I lay beside Murray on the lumpy mattress with the sounds of the girls' soft breathing just a few feet away, I felt overwhelmed with gratitude. I was so deeply thankful that Dad's prognosis was positive. I was poignantly aware that if he lived in Aiud, he would, at the young age of sixty-one, most probably be dead.

• • •

We worked hard during that trip and saw great progress on the renovation of the clinic. In addition to our labor, we made sure we had some fun too. We took trips to the countryside to enjoy its vast beauty. One of the jaw-dropping places our Romanian friends proudly took us to was Cheile Râmeţului.

We set out early one Saturday morning with a picnic. After a fairly tenuous drive along mud roads, where several of us were somewhat carsick from the sharp, hairpin curves and bumps along the route, we finally came to a halt. The road had quite literally ended. We abandoned our overcrowded cars and began to walk to our destination. Our hike took us through a steep ravine, where we had to hold on to ropes so we wouldn't fall into raging waters. We carried huge amounts of food for the picnic, including massive sacks filled with bread. Romanians have a saying: *"dacă nu aţi mâncat pâine, n-ai mâncat."* This translates to "If you haven't eaten bread, you haven't eaten." If there wasn't oodles of bread, and I mean OODLES, there was no party to be had.

Romanians are a traditional and family-oriented people. Everyone attends picnics, from the tiny newborn babies to the oldest grannies. It was quite an accomplishment to get all of us and our large quantity of vittles and other trappings to the picnic spot carefully chosen for its grandeur and beauty. Our little girls rode on strong shoulders through the ravine and squealed with pure delight the entire way.

Our Romanian friends knew how to have simple fun, with lots of music and laughter and copious amounts of delicious food. One of the locals had recently slaughtered a pig, so in addition to the aforementioned bread, we feasted on scrumptious pork schnitzel. This was accompanied by a side of Romanian salad consisting of tomatoes, cucumbers, garlic, and red onions in a zesty vinaigrette. It was all made onsite with frighteningly sharp knives that magically appeared from apron pockets. There was an inordinate selection of delectable homemade pastries and sweets to finish off too. That day, we enjoyed a truly scrumptious feast.

Wildflowers exhibited their beauty all around us, and my very creative Victoria became an expert at making daisy chain tiaras for herself, Julia, and anyone else who would consent to wear them, male or female. Musicians played guitars and loud singing spontaneously erupted throughout the afternoon. Before long, the old men were laying out flat on the meadow grass, raucously snoring. They had been tippling on *țuică*, a bootleg plum brandy. A few sips of that triple distilled firewater was enough to knock anyone off their feet.

I would wager that it was one of the most brilliant picnics I had ever enjoyed. No wonder I loved this country. The generosity and kindness of its people were second to none.

· · ·

Romanians are very artistic. I met many amazing painters, sculptors, ceramic artists, woodworkers, and lace-needlework experts, to name a few. We regularly took our teams to visit local artisans so they could buy beautiful artifacts as souvenirs and gifts. No matter what time of day or night we visited people in their homes, they treated us to their exceptional hospitality. There was no such thing as a quick visit. Food would miraculously appear within seconds of our arrival. It was always accompanied by a bottle of homemade țuică. We learned quickly that it was just plain bad manners to refuse this prized alcoholic beverage. Traditional țuică is 40 to 45 percent alcohol by volume (some as high as 65 percent), so one small glass was adequate for my lightweight frame.

Unfortunately, there was never just a single pour. Once the first glass was downed, the stopper would pop within a split second and the next glass would materialize. There was no outfoxing our generous hosts by nursing the first glass. They had all the time in the world for their honored guests and would politely wait for hours for that second pour.

Quickly, we realized it was best to make these visits at the end of a day rather than in the early morning. Țuică was no respecter of time. It was poured at any time of day or night. Drinking firewater at nine a.m. was quite a nasty way to start your day. I still gag ever so slightly when I think about trying to consume the stuff in the morning.

• • •

Good hygiene wasn't always attainable. Many homes did not have refrigerators, but food was never wasted. If it was not eaten the first day, it was set aside for the next day, or the next, or the next. Frequently, it was not refrigerated during that time. Often the water service was cut off for hours, so hands were not always washed. On several occasions during our years in Aiud, there were typhoid outbreaks. We had to be very careful.

On one of our trips, Julia and I came down with a particularly nasty stomach bug. By the time we arrived back in Paisley, we still weren't back to normal. Any food we ate ran right through us. Since our condition wasn't improving, I decided that a visit to the doctor was in order. I explained to my doctor what was going on, and she put us on antibiotics.

The following day, I had just arrived home from picking Victoria up from school when I heard pounding on my front door. Recently, our flat had been broken into, so the hammering on our door made me jumpy. We had been robbed twice within a month, both times while I was out picking the girls up from school. Nervously, I squinted through the peephole. On the opposite side of it stood a friendly looking woman. I cracked open the door to greet her, keeping the safety bolt in place. Why was she craning her head around me to look into the flat?

"Can I help you?" I asked a little brusquely.

"I am from the health department," she said as she pulled out her credentials. "I work in the division that cares for high-risk children. I am here today for a home visit because the results from your child's tests show a bacteria that is usually only found in conditions of squalor. I need to check on the cleanliness of your home and the safety of your child," she said as she continued to peer through the crack in the door. "But, from what I can see, your house looks very tidy. I am a bit perplexed. May I come in and look around?"

I slid back the bolt and invited her in. I explained that we had just returned from a trip to Romania, where we had picked up the nasty bug. She was very apologetic and relieved that all was safe and well for Julia. I was suitably impressed by the speed of Britain's National Health Service. With a little more kindness in my voice, I thanked her profusely for coming to check up on Julia. I had not even heard back from my doctor's office with the results, but a red flag had been raised at the lab, causing the powers protecting children to snap into action.

Thanks to the antibiotics, we were feeling better and back to full health in no time. I was freshly aware, once again, how fortunate we were to live in a country where there is wonderful health care. We had antibiotics the instant we needed them, and someone had even come to check on us. I wondered how many three-year-olds in Romania were living with infections and bugs that did not get treatment. Probably a lot. We were indeed lucky. This thought echoed in my brain for days.

CHAPTER 10

· · · · · · · · · · · · · · · · · ·

Poppy Fields and The Ice Machine Hotel

I don't remember how many volunteer teams we took into Romania over the next couple of years, but there were definitely quite a few. Soon, Murray and I became aware of a new idea niggling away in the back of our minds. It was becoming increasingly difficult to work in our regular jobs in Scotland while doing all our work in Romania. Perhaps we should leave Scotland and move to Romania? What!? Where had that crazy thought come from? We couldn't believe we were even contemplating such a ridiculous notion. But this thought just kept worming its way around in our minds, forcing us to give it serious consideration. We could not silence the idea, no matter how we tried.

Murray and I looked at it logically. There were many really good reasons to relocate to Romania. There was so much to do there. On the other hand, there were a lot of reasons why it could be outright folly. What about the girls' education? They were four and six now. How would we earn money to live? Where would we find a place to live in a town that had a severe housing shortage. We didn't own a vehicle, so how would we even get there? This idea of living in Romania was ludicrous. What the hell were we thinking?

The niggle continued to grow. It became a whisper. It gradually grew into a very loud voice inside each of us. We couldn't shake it. We had done some crazy things and seen amazing miracles unfold when we needed them most. Why should this be any different? Why would we not move forward just because we could imagine a few obstacles?

In early 1993, we finally stopped grappling with the idea and decided to move to Romania. We let all our friends and family know. They had been supportive of our decisions over the past few years, and we would need their continued help and support to make this work. We canvased family and friends in New Zealand, Canada, and the UK for more financial assistance to help cover our anticipated monthly expenses. Amazingly, we saw a marked increase in our monthly income, despite the fact that we no longer had "paying" jobs.

In the late spring, I flew out to Aiud for a few days to search for a place to live. Becky and Dorin had married a few months earlier, and Becky had recently moved to live in Aiud and work in the new clinic as a doctor. Ever-helpful Dorin explored every avenue imaginable to help find us housing, but to no avail. I incorrectly assumed I would easily find us a place to live. After all, if we were meant to move there, then something would become available for us. I searched all around the town with Dorin, trying to find somewhere to rent. Nothing!

On the last day before I was scheduled to return to Scotland, Dorin came home with welcome news. He thought he may have found a house for me and my family and suggested I have a look at it. He warned me that it was not ideal, but it was all he could find after weeks of searching. Hmm. When a Romanian suggests "not ideal," that means it's probably pretty bad. This did not sound great, but it was all there was. So off we went. The home was very old and fairly run down, as many homes in the town were. It was situated on a large picturesque lot that I rather liked. The owner was a single woman. The house had been in her family for generations. She and her young daughter lived there now. She quickly showed us the part of her house that was available for lease. It had two small rooms with a separate entrance from the main house. Next to these rooms was a tiny closetlike space with a sink. She was quite sure we could turn the closet into a functioning kitchen if we could bring a small fridge and stove with us. I had my doubts. I tried not to do an eyeroll, but one creeped out before I could stop it. There was a tiny bathroom located outside at the end of the porch. She assured me that it was completely functional and would be ours to use exclusively. It had a toilet and bathtub which had seen better days. No sink. Hmm. What did I think? She enthusiastically assured me she would love to rent it to us for a very good price. Describing this "house" as basic was somewhat of an understatement. But I had found absolutely nothing else, so I decided to go with the flow and agreed to rent it. I was pretty sure we could find a way to make it work. After all, I was becoming a master of making the most of small and awkward spaces.

Our new landlady had the two rooms jampacked with junk. They were bursting with stuff. Scarcely a square inch was vacant. She explained it was presently her storage space for everything that her family had acquired over several generations. I did not doubt it. Decades of deprivation meant that people never threw anything away. They hoarded everything because they never knew what items would be available in the future. Clearly that is the case here, I thought as I surveyed the towers of junk in front of me. Bunny trails ran through the mountains of clutter to beds that were groaning with disgust from the sheer weight of family treasures piled high upon them. She assured me that the rooms would be emptied before we arrived back in a few weeks. I foolishly believed her, paid a deposit, shook her hand, and returned home the next day. I was thankful to have finally found somewhere my family could live when we returned to Aiud in a few weeks.

Next, we focused on what we would do with our flat while away. No problem there. We quickly found three delightful young women who worked for the nonprofit in Scotland. They rented out our place, which would take care of the mortgage. Well that was easy.

Then we looked into schooling for the girls. We weren't happy about putting them into the school system in Romania. They did not speak any Romanian. At that time, the Romanian education system still ran on old school Communist ideas that were very punitive. Recently, we had learned that Victoria had mild dyslexia. We did not want to aggravate this learning disability by having her in a non-English speaking punitive educational environment. We didn't want Julia in this environment either. So we considered homeschooling as an option. We had no idea where to begin. I was discussing this dilemma on the phone with my parents when they suggested I look into The Correspondence School in New Zealand.

I had not known of the school's existence until my parents mentioned it. I made some phone calls and quickly learned that it was New Zealand's largest school. Each year, about 25,000 pupils were enrolled in classes from early childhood through high school. Its reputation for high-quality education was second to none.

The New Zealand government founded the school in 1922 as a "a school for the benefit of the most isolated children, for example of lighthouse keepers and remote shepherds living upon small islands or in mountainous districts." Historical documents described it as "a school of last resort, ensuring that no matter where he lived every New Zealand child should have as full an education as he was capable of achieving."

Nowadays, the school offered a full and free education to New Zealand children who not only lived in isolated rural locations in New Zealand but also to those Kiwi kids who lived in non-English speaking countries. We immediately applied for the girls to "attend" this school, and they were accepted because they fulfilled the criteria.

I will forever be thankful to New Zealand for this amazing school and the education it afforded my daughters. The girls were assigned teachers, and we began their new schooling even before we left Scotland. These were still pretty early days for computers, so even though a little of the correspondence was done via email, most of the schoolwork still required books, journals, and so on. Twice a month, we received a couple of large boxes full of all the materials the girls needed for their classes. There were workbooks for every subject and instruction booklets for their supervisor. There was a multitude of other materials, like science equipment, educational toys, items for experiments, and loads and loads of library books. It was an incredible outfit with amazing resources.

It was like Christmas twice a month for the girls. We visited the post office to pick up our large boxes. At the same time, we returned their completed work for the teachers to review. In each new box, the teachers would return the graded work from the previous month, along with new materials for the next couple of weeks. The New Zealand government paid for everything.

To this day, my daughters still possess some of the brilliant writings and projects they did during their correspondence schooling. Not too long ago, we looked through some of their work. It was fascinating to see that the things they wrote about as children in Romania were now reflected in the careers they pursued in later life. But I digress.

In 1993, it was still difficult to purchase household items in Romania. We would have to take with us everything we needed for the girls and for our home. This would require a vehicle. We did not own a car and could not see a solution to this problem. We had no savings, and our limited income from our part-time jobs had just ended. Credit was unavailable to us. We just couldn't work out a solution. We knew we needed a miracle. We set a date for our departure and gathered everything we anticipated we would need to take with us to Romania. We had seen miracles in the past, and we knew we would see them again.

A week before we were due to depart, a friend who knew we needed a vehicle dropped by to visit us. He told us of a friend who had a very old Land Rover that was in need of work. He hadn't driven it in a very long time. He would attempt to get it running again and donate it to us. Since we had nothing else, it sounded perfect. A few days later, and just a couple of days prior to our planned departure, our friend pulled up to our flat with a veritable Land Rover relic. This thing was unquestionably old and extremely dirty inside and out. But it was running. Despite its condition, we felt so much gratitude for this answer to our need. When we rolled up to the carwash, the attendants were appalled at the state of the car. They muttered things like "should have got it cleaned before you returned from safari" and "hours of work" while they shot us murderous glances and told us not to come back for a few hours. It really was a sight to behold. Unquestionably, they had every reason to be chagrined.

A couple of days later, we loaded up our now buffed-up relic. Murray, the packing maestro, waved his magic wand over the vehicle. Once again, I was mesmerized by how much he packed into such a small space. It truly was a work of art.

And so in the fall of 1993, we spluttered along our way, out of Paisley and across Europe, to start our next adventure in a very old, green Land Rover that the girls had by now lovingly named Grover, a portmanteau of green and rover. Unfortunately, Grover was so old that he did not care too much for long hot days and had to take frequent rests.

On our fourth day of driving, just as we were chugging past fields crimson with poppies on our approach into Budapest, Grover sputtered and came to a complete stop. We opened the hood and peered in. Neither Murray nor I have any mechanical ability, so we did not have the slightest clue what we were looking at. Mobile phones were not ubiquitous yet, so Murray commenced to hitchhike twenty miles to Budapest to find the nearest garage to get the assistance we needed.

I didn't know how long we'd be waiting, so I set up a picnic in a field of poppies beside the busy highway. I pulled out a blanket and some food for the girls. Out came their dollies to sit beside them and enjoy a splendid picnic on a lovely summer's day. Despite the pretty picture, I felt just a hair anxious about our safety. We were vulnerable "rich Westerners" sitting there on the side of a Hungarian highway. Poverty in Eastern Europe was still widespread. We were an easy target for any unsavory passerby looking for an opportunity.

I prayed we would be invisible and everything would be okay. I hoped that Murray would get this situation sorted out quickly and without too much difficulty. I tried to stay calm for the kids' sake, but I was quite nervous about the whole damn situation. A few hours later, I saw the tow truck approaching with Murray waving at us from the passenger seat. I sighed in relief. I may have done thirty seconds worth of pogo-stick type jumps too. I could no longer contain my joy at the return of my shining knight in the rescue vehicle.

Murray and the tow truck driver hooked Grover up to the truck while the girls and I packed up the dollies and the picnic. We all piled into the truck and headed for our first of many trips into beautiful Budapest. On our arrival at the garage, and after some serious peering at things under the hood, the mechanic diagnosed Grover with a serious illness. He told us it would take a couple of days to make him well again. There was no quick fix, so it was time to find somewhere to stay.

As luck would have it, right across the road from the garage stood a brand-new hotel. It was almost shocking to see this new Western-style construction, especially when everything else around was historic and run down. But there it stood, bright, shiny, and new, beckoning us in.

We trundled across the road, dragging along a huge pile of luggage. We didn't think it wise to leave our belongings in the vehicle, so we had to make several trips back and forth to the hotel to make sure that Grover was empty. We must have been quite a sight, inquiring about a room with our mountain of belongings behind us. Thank goodness there did not appear to be too many other people around. I didn't really like being a spectacle, which clearly we were.

The desk clerk merrily told us that the hotel had opened a few days prior and there were plenty of rooms available. As we were checking in, the manager popped out of his office to greet us as though we were long-lost friends. With a viselike grip shake of our hands, he said he would like to welcome us with a complimentary upgrade to a suite. That was before he spotted the mound of gear behind us in the lobby. We could have definitely been mistaken for squatters, so before he could change his mind, I grabbed the key card from his hand, gave him a big thank you hug—best to throw him off his game!—and jumped into the elevator and whizzed straight up to the top floor.

Our girls were elated with their new digs. Their favorite activity was running along the vacant corridor to the ice machine and collecting copious quantities of ice, whether we wanted it or not. Our new lodging was dubbed "The Ice Machine Hotel" by our Captain Obvious daughters. They wormed their way into the heart of the hotel manager's wife and made frequent trips to her suite to play with her kitties and eat cookies.

Eastern European outfits weren't known for rapid service, and the garage across the street was no exception. Four days later, after a most restful stay in our suite, Grover was finally in passable health again. He would get us over the border into Romania, the wiry mechanic assured us. Time for the repacking event. Our astonishing performance caused a lot of wide-mouthed gawking from the hotel guests and staff. I got it. We weren't your everyday tourists, carrying normal touristy things. Nonetheless, we got the royal goodbye wave from the hotel manager and the entire staff as we piled back into Grover and set off for the final eight-hour leg of our journey to Aiud. It crossed my mind that they might have just been pleased to see us go, hence the hearty farewell. But the manager assured us we were welcome back anytime. We might have been a bit of an enigma to him, truth be told . . . like when you try to stop looking at a disaster scene, but just can't help yourself!

I know it's a bit trite to say, but what sometimes appears to be a bad situation can actually be a blessing, and this was truly one of those times. I had felt so upset about Grover breaking down. We really did not have the wherewithal to fix him. In addition, we hadn't planned on a four-night stay in a hotel, and it ate into resources that we needed for living in Romania. It was really scary sitting out there on the road alone with the girls, waiting for Murray's return, but it had brought us to that wonderful resting place in Budapest where we met the loveliest hotel manager imaginable. For the next few years, when we needed to take time away from the dirt, dust, and exhaustion we sometimes felt in Romania, "The Ice Machine Hotel" was our go-to place. The manager always gave us an upgraded suite. It was like our little oasis in the desert. Who would have thought when I was anxiously waiting by the side of the road just outside of Budapest, worrying about our safety, that this little hiccup in our travel would result in a wonderful long-term treat?

Now, when I go through difficult times, I try to remember such experiences. I remind myself that the next struggle or difficulty is no different from struggles in the past. I know the *power of things unseen*. I know to have faith. I know to hold tight. I know to believe in miracles and that good comes from difficulty. This power is an unending source from which I can draw. I have learned that I will never be in a situation that is beyond what I can cope with. Strength and help are always available to me in times of need.

CHAPTER 11

· · · · · · · · · · · · · · · · ·

Speckle's Demise and Mushroom Pixies

Crossing the border into Romania was very time consuming and somewhat nerve-racking. We had visas which allowed us to live and work for a nonprofit in Romania. However, that meant little to the border police who acted as though they were the judge, jury, and executioners. Many of these men had been Ceaușescu's Securitate, so they were well versed in using fear to get what they wanted. Initially, I found them quite scary. They rifled through our vehicle, picking out all the things they wanted. They then demanded money. The first couple of times this happened, we immediately gave into their bullying and handed over our greenbacks along with the other items they had purloined from the vehicle. But we eventually grew bolder and pushed back. A funny thing happened when we did: Our lack of subservience frightened them into being kinder and less demanding. Our fear fueled their mean behavior. But when we responded with strength, they stepped back and allowed us through. This was a fascinating lesson. Looking back, I realized that the same thing happened on that horrible day at Otopeni Airport when the girls and I were detained. The guards quickly backed down once I stood up to them.

This particular trip was only the second time we crossed the border from Hungary into Romania in a vehicle. Unfortunately, we had not yet learned to stand up to the guards, so we allowed them to relieve us of a few of our belongings and gave them money. Once through the checkpoint, we rumbled past the massive, polluting power plant in Oradea toward Aiud. We traversed the simply stunning countryside, winding our way through quaint villages, past fields dotted with fairytalelike haystacks, en route to our destination.

We rolled into Aiud as it neared sunset. I jumped from our vehicle and swung open the gates. Murray pulled into our new yard amidst a flurry of clucking chickens flying all around us. Victoria and Julia jumped out of Grover, excited to have finally arrived at their new home after our nine-day journey. They were quite delighted by the picturesque yard with all its wildlife. In addition to the aforementioned chickens, pigs grunted in their pens, kittens skittered underfoot, and dogs raucously yipped at our heels. It was a stunningly beautiful late summer's evening. Magnificent sunflowers, laden with seeds, bowed their heads as the butterflies and hummingbirds floated around them. It crossed my mind that we had stepped into one of Beatrix Potter's Bunnykins scenes. *Perhaps this new home will work out better than I anticipated, I thought.*

But my heart dropped to the bottom of my shoes when I opened the door to our two rooms. I just couldn't believe the scene before my eyes. The landlady hadn't removed a thing. She had just rearranged the junk so that it was lining the walls in neater piles. It was still total chaos in there and a totally unacceptable living arrangement. I felt sick. Murray, who had followed me into the rooms, raised an eyebrow and let out a low whistle. He did not say a thing, but the corners of his mouth twitched.

I looked up and saw the owner rushing down the dirt yard toward us, gesticulating wildly. On her arrival at our living quarters, she breathlessly explained that she had found absolutely nowhere she could move her belongings to, so the only option was for us to share the space with her junk. She explained that she had worked hard to remove the junk piles from the cheerlessly sagging beds. She smiled broadly as she clarified this meant they were now vacant for our use. Astonishingly, she appeared to be pretty chuffed with her efforts. She was delusionally positive that this was an acceptable solution.

Was she freaking kidding me? My heart rate skyrocketed as I argued with her that this was not the arrangement we made a few weeks back. I reminded her that she had assured me the rooms would be empty on our arrival. By now, I noticed Murray had wisely returned back to the garden bliss with the girls to chase butterflies.

Our landlady was totally undaunted by my outrage. She argued back, telling me there was nothing she could do to make it better for us. Our discussion went in circles, the volume rising with each go-round. She suggested, quite ridiculously, that we should be pleased with our new home. I felt as though steam was coming out of my ears.

"Haven't you had weeks to clear out your junk?" came my retort once again. "That was our arrangement."

She just kept shaking her head, arms crossed in front of her, mouth drawn. We were quite clearly at loggerheads. She would not budge, and I certainly could not be convinced these were acceptable living conditions. This conversation was going nowhere. I harrumphed, crossed my arms, and stared back at her.

We were at a standstill. These rooms were all we had right now, and continuing to argue with her was not the immediate answer. We had been traveling for hours and were all very tired. Any further discussion was futile. So I zipped my mouth shut. She turned and headed back up the yard to her part of the house. "Be sure to let me know if there is anything you need," she called over her shoulder as she left. Visions of a trash heap full of her belongings danced in my aching head, but I held my tongue for once.

We would sort this out somehow. But not tonight. So with no further ado, I summoned Murray and the girls back to our new residence, where we had no choice but to make do for now. We unpacked Grover and piled all our belongings in a massive pile on the porch. There was no room inside for even one of our boxes. I expected that we could find a way to sort this out the following day. Little did I realize how futile that hope was.

Nothing I could say over the following days mattered. Our landlady would not move her belongings from our living space. It was terrible. But there were just no other living options available and life had to go on, so we coped the best we could. We set up school at a little table that we managed to clear of her junk. We cooked meals in the tiny space allotted to us as our kitchen. We attempted to take baths when the water unexpectedly came on for a few hours each day. We learned to fill all the containers we possessed with water, because we never knew when we would next have water.

It was easier to spend most of our time outside in the lovely yard rather than trying to cope with the disaster inside. The outdoors soon became the schoolroom, the dining room, and even the living room. I prefer my living space to be ordered, so living in someone else's junk just about sent me over the edge. At least I did not have to look at her junk when I was outside, and I took pleasure in the beauty of nature surrounding me. But no matter how much I tried to find the positive, I was still stressed by this far from ideal situation. It was hard not to let my mind doubt our decision to move to Romania. I was poignantly aware that the garden escape could not last forever, especially with winter looming around the corner. We continued our new home search with gusto because we had to find somewhere better very soon.

. . .

I really love food. Anyone who knows me will vouch for that. I especially love trying all sorts of different ethnic food, and particularly so if it is healthy fare. It is a rare occasion that I won't try something new at least once. I've eaten chicken feet, cow's tongue, sheep's stomach, and pig's testicles, to name a few. Even though I am not about to make those dishes my weekly staples anytime soon, I enjoyed trying all of them once and found them strangely intriguing experiences.

But I had no idea quite what I was getting myself into when the landlady invited us to share dinner with her and her daughter. I was still at a stalemate with her about our unsatisfactory living arrangement, and I was not feeling too warm and fuzzy toward her. "Maybe a leisurely dinner together will help us sort this out," I mused to Murray. He nodded in agreement and smiled.

It was a balmy Saturday afternoon, and we sat together in the garden enjoying the obligatory dram of țuică that kicked off all social events. Victoria and Julia were in the garden playing with a black kitten that had recently turned up. They had named her Pepsi, and she was already wearing dolly clothes. The chickens were clucking around us, pecking morsels and bugs from the rich soil. The girls had made fast friends with the chickens, and they named an especially tame one "Speckles." Speckles would let them pick her up and cuddle her. I could see that before long, my pet-whispering children would have Speckles dressed in dolly clothes, wrapped in a blanket, and tucked into their dolly pram right beside Pepsi!

I was pleased for this relaxing afternoon with our landlady and very hopeful we could get to the topic of her junk. She appeared to be in a good mood, perhaps helped along by the țuică that flowed seamlessly into her glass. After about an hour of happy idle chat, I was ready to steer the conversation toward our living quarters. I had just summoned the energy to talk about this when our host stood up and informed us she was going to prepare dinner. Suddenly, before we had any idea what she was doing, she grabbed the unsuspecting Speckles, whipped out a knife, and chopped off her head on a stump of wood just a few feet away from us. Exactly one second later, my poor sensitive Victoria keeled over in a dead faint and Julia started howling. I could hardly believe what had just transpired right in front of our noses. It was like a scene from your worst nightmare. Speckles's warm body was twitching and oozing vital fluids as the landlady held her blood-dripping head high in the air like a trophy. Murray and I immediately tried to revive and calm the girls, but the shocking scene was not helping us. The chicken murderer's fingers began working at record speed, creating a frenzy of feathers flying through the air until Speckles was stark naked. All the while she regaled us in Romanian (which I hardly understood due to my poor language-learning skills and the shock of the situation) that if we were going to live in Romania, we had to get used to real life. Fainting and crying over a little animal blood was silly.

I was absolutely furious with her for inflicting this on my daughters. I was valiantly trying to hold myself back from knocking her to the ground all the while trying to soothe the girls. They were really distressed by the horror that had just unfolded before their innocent eyes.

I attempted to calm myself, aware that an all-out lady brawl in front of my distressed kids would not help the ghoulish situation. Then I realized something that made me quite uncomfortable. Our landlady had generously killed her fattest chicken to share with us for dinner. She had kindly sacrificed her very best fowl for us, which unfortunately meant we couldn't just walk away and I certainly could not knock her to the ground. Despite the trauma suffered by the girls, we had to show gratitude to our landlady for her generosity. Somehow we would have to consume Speckles when she was served up to us on a platter.

Thank goodness it was going to take a couple of hours until Speckles was ready for human consumption. We could calm down and work out how best to deal with this rather bizarre affair. We needed to get out of the yard because there was still a haze of feathers wafting around in the twilight, blood pooling around our feet, and a chicken head lying on a stump. It was a grizzly scene. We needed to escape to somewhere as far away from the killing fields as possible.

We uncreatively made up a story that the girls were tired and weren't used to eating dinner so late. Since it was only about six p.m., this was completely unbelievable. But in the heat of the moment, it was the best we could do. As we scuttled away, I unceremoniously announced to our host that just Murray and I would come to her kitchen once the girls were settled into bed.

We arrived in her kitchen an hour or so later and were greeted by an appalling smell emanating from the stove. I could see Speckles frying in a pan. On the stove right next to our befriended chicken, a large pot that looked suspiciously like a witch's cauldron furiously bubbled away. I suspected this was where the foul aroma radiated from, mostly because I knew it was certainly something other than the smell of frying poultry assaulting my nostrils.

I ungraciously enquired about the contents of the cauldron and was informed it was our first course. It was a delicacy our landlady had prepared especially in our honor.

"Oh yes," I said, trying not to gag at the odor and attempting not to be so mean-spirited despite the macabre events of the day. *Focus on kindness,* I whispered in my roiling head.

"Rice boiled in fresh pig's blood," she said. At that moment, I felt a little bile bubble up into my throat.

She ladled it into a bowl and passed it over to me. It was a brown glutinous mess, and I just knew I could not consume it, no matter how rude it seemed. Even the smell brought me perilously close to vomiting. Speckles now looked positively delicious!

There is a first for everything, and I do believe this was the first time I just didn't care how offensive I was being to another human being who showed great kindness to me. I couldn't eat the cauldron goop, and I quietly handed the untouched plate back to her. After the proceedings earlier in the day, I had passed the point where I cared anymore. I kind of disliked our landlady anyway and trying to be polite was in the too-hard basket at that exact moment. Clearly we were a bad fit.

I left her kitchen that disastrous night cognizant of the fact that our stay at this home was not turning out to be a roaring success. It was definitely time to elevate the "new home" search to top gear.

It is a meal I will never soon forget, perhaps because of the Speckles event. Interestingly, I never saw that particular rice dish again anywhere in Romania, and we ate many dishes at many different places. I asked several of my Romanian friends about it over the years, but no one seemed to have heard of this dish. This led me to secretly believe my landlady was actually trying to eliminate us and blame it on natural causes.

No matter what the real story is, it was a "delicacy" that I was happy to never encounter again. Bizarrely, chicken is still my favorite dish and I have to fess up: Speckles was absolutely scrumptious!

• • •

After that unfortunate encounter, we indeed knew we needed to move lickety-split. On many levels, it just wasn't working. One crisp fall day, Dorin arrived at our house with news about an entire house that was vacant and available for rent. There was no such thing as a classifieds section in the local paper. Everything was word of mouth. This news from Dorin's lips was heaven sent.

"Take me now!" I squealed. I jumped a little, inducing a giggle from the girls. School was instantaneously dismissed. I herded my pupils and Dorin into Grover in less than a microsecond, hit the gas, and arrived at the indicated address in short order.

An Englishman with Romanian roots owned the house. He had bought it a year before and had begun renovating it. The process had not gone as easily as he hoped, so he had abandoned his plans for relocation and returned to the UK. Word on the street was that he now wanted a good tenant. I was ecstatic. We sent word along that we would love to rent his house. I could not wait to say toodle-oo to the chicken-murderer. This was a godsend.

Even though it was only partially renovated and somewhat ramshackle, it was a proper home. We would not have to share space with another person's junk, and we had room to unpack our belongings that were still languishing in boxes on the porch.

We had moved to Aiud, in part, so that we could more easily plan, organize, and host regular volunteer teams working on our medical and educational projects. This had been almost impossible to do at the chicken-murderer's house. A larger home with better facilities was imperative. This house, even with its limitations, would work.

The kitchen was in usable shape, the house was heated, and there was even a real bathroom. We had cold running water most of the time. Since the house had no water heater, we boiled large pots of water on the stove and carried them through to the bathtub in order to bathe. This was a great improvement over the washcloth and basin method we'd employed at our previous lodging. We had three large, pristine, and wonderful empty rooms to make our home. Indisputably, we still weren't residing at the Ritz-Carlton, but we were making bold progress. We were so very thankful and more than a little relieved to move into our new digs before the full force of winter hit.

• • •

It was a herculean task to procure food in those first couple of years. There was a weekly farmers' market, which had great produce during the summer. But by the time winter rolled in, there were just a few hardy farmers trying to sell the last of their wizened potatoes, carrots, and onions that they had preserved in a cold cellar. In the depths of winter, we learned that even this mummified produce was a hot commodity.

Romanian friends taught me that I could purchase fresh cow's milk by visiting the farmers' market every Thursday morning at four thirty. Here I met a tiny old woman farmer who came down from the mountains on her mule once a week to sell rich creamy milk. A four-thirty appointment wasn't too bad during the summertime, but it felt a bit onerous in winter when the clock alarm rocked us out of our deep slumber. As I crawled out from under my warm bedsheets, I grumbled about how difficult it was to procure something as simple as milk. But when I climbed into Grover, it didn't take long to remember just how lucky I was. I had a vehicle. I could drive the few miles to market and home again. Many of Aiud's residents did not own cars and had to walk to market in the frigid temperatures and then carry the milk home. It really became about perspective and choosing to be thankful.

The creamy, frothy milk, known as bivolița was always fresh. The farmer poured the almost-warm milk out of her large metal cans and into the empty soda bottles I brought with me to market. As this milk was not pasteurized, I took further action to ensure its safety for consumption. Once I returned home, I poured it into a huge pot, boiled it hard for several minutes, and then let it cool. Some of it went right into the refrigerator, and some I froze. I learned to stockpile milk for the days when the old farmer didn't turn up.

• • •

One of my more difficult jobs was providing meals for our teams. This required generous quantities of food. It took a great deal of time to find even basic foodstuffs. It was almost a full-time job in itself.

But we knew how lucky we were compared to our Romanian friends. We could come and go from Romania as we pleased because we were foreign and had a vehicle. We frequently visited Hungary on food-buying sorties. Debrecen was the closest Hungarian city to us, and it had so many more goods and services available than in Aiud. It felt bounteous when we went into the stores. We always stocked up on an amazing assortment of goods, particularly humongous quantities of food.

I still remember our excitement on one of those visits when we stumbled across a small chest freezer in a newly opened appliance store. They were selling "Western-imported appliances." Though it was exorbitantly overpriced, we purchased it with far more excitement than a mundane freezer deserved. We tied it onto our roof rack and returned to Aiud. It was promptly and most stupidly dubbed the "adorable freezer." Life was much easier, just because we could stockpile food over the summer for the coming winter.

Apart from the bakeries selling Romanian bread, food stores in Aiud were totally barren most of the time. Nada. Not a thing. Zilch. It was crazy searching for food and finding shelves totally devoid of anything except perhaps țuică—not exactly the nourishment I wanted to feed my family and guests.

Occasionally, we heard news through the grapevine that a particular store was expecting a delivery of salami or some other food product on a certain day. The entire town would drop everything it was doing and rush out the door. A throng of hopeful souls would converge on the store, only to find about ten strings of lonely looking salami hanging in an otherwise empty store. These foodstuffs were often at unaffordable prices for most people. It was awful to see folks just standing there, lustfully staring at the few precious sticks of salami. Our United States currency spoke volumes, and we were among the fortunate few who could purchase these overpriced treasures, providing food for our visiting volunteer teams.

On other occasions, word reached us that someone in the town was about to slaughter a pig or a cow. We would hotfoot it to the house where this was about to take place. We often got first dibs on the choice cuts, because everyone wanted our precious US money. I purchased a mincer and quickly became an expert at making my own hamburger meat. It went a lot further when feeding our hungry volunteer teams. I became proficient at cutting up huge slabs of meat into more manageable chunks. We'd then drop them into our absurdly "adorable freezer," where they joined the huge quantities of summer produce. These seemingly small blessings were massive.

• • •

When mushroom season arrived, my friend Marta—the most energetic grandmother I had ever met—took me under her wing. She led a small group of the womenfolk, including her precious grandkids, my girls, and me, to the forest to gather fungi. This was serious business, mostly because you had to know exactly which ones were safe to eat, and which ones were fatally toxic. Marta informed me there are about sixty toxic varieties of mushrooms in Romania. Quite a few people die each year from eating highly poisonous mushrooms they have mistaken for tasty morels.

With great trepidation, I learned the art of mushroom differentiation from this all-knowing grandma who had done this every year of her life and was still here to tell her tale. She checked every single mushroom we collected. She was amazing. She could see the minuscule differences indicating which mushrooms were good and which were not. I implicitly trusted her knowledge. When she said "Keep," we kept, and when she said "Throw," we threw. The girls absolutely loved mushroom day. It was such a fun outing, strolling through the forest with our sacks on our backs on a crisp fall day. It felt like a fairytale moment, as though a pixie would appear from under one of the huge smoky colored mushrooms. It certainly beat sitting at home doing schoolwork, and yet it was education with a twist.

Marta knew the best location and the exact day to collect fungi. She took us deep into the forest at the crack of dawn. It was an all-day adventure with picnic and all. We returned home at the end of a long day with sacks bulging full of many delectable varieties. Mushroom season was very short, but somehow she knew the perfect moment to head for the forest. The supplies were plentiful if you embarked at the right time.

She taught me how to store our prized collection on our return home. The first job was worm extrication. This was the girls' duty and resulted in much squealing and laughter. We would then wash them thoroughly and blanch them in boiling water. Once they had cooled, we squeezed all the moisture out of them until they appeared to be dehydrated. We would finally drop them into the "adorable freezer," which always found room for Marta's stash as well. *Voilà!* We had mushrooms for the next several months from just one long, fun day of foraging among the pixies in the forest. My knowledge bank of survival techniques just kept growing. We were all getting an education.

CHAPTER 12

. . . .

Candy and Excited Grunting Pigs

A reliable vehicle was essential for our work. To our dismay, Grover was unequal to the task. One day he just turned up his heels and gave up the ghost. Romanians have a knack for fixing almost anything, so when our mechanic issued a death sentence on Grover, we initiated his last rites.

Fortuitously, we were about to embark on a two-week fundraising trip back to the UK the following week. Since we had no vehicle for the trip, we flew.

During this trip, we met a truly wonderful family named the Scotts, indisputably the most appropriate name for a family of Scots. They lived on a large and beautiful estate in Dumfries and Galloway. They invited us to stay in their mews for a few days of R and R.

One evening over dinner, the topic of Land Rovers came up. The Scotts had owned Land Rovers for many years and were enthusiastic champions of these workhorses. We regaled our new friends with tales of Grover's exploits in Romania. It was the perfect country for a rugged 4WD, and they much enjoyed hearing about Grover's feats.

A few days prior to our planned return to Romania, the Scotts called us. They had an almost-new twelve-seater diesel Land Rover Defender they wished to donate to us for our work in Romania. Even though we had hoped for a miracle, we could hardly fathom just how perfect this Land Rover was for our needs. We were overwhelmed with gratitude. People we hadn't even known a couple of weeks earlier stepped forward and became our angels. Suddenly, all the difficult challenges we faced in our work just seemed to get a little bit easier.

Our shiny new Land Rover was bright red and white, so the girls suitably named her Candy. We had a new skip in our step as we loaded her up and once again tootled off to Romania. This time I was not stressed about making the long journey in an unreliable vehicle. We suffered no breakdowns on the side of the road, and I felt such a sense of peace. The *power of things unseen* once again amazed me.

I am not sure the Scotts will ever know just how much their exceptionally generous gift contributed to the success of our work. Our "new" car was often jammed full of teams heading off to work projects or outings, or loaded with supplies to be distributed. She was a hard worker during those years in Romania.

On one Saturday afternoon, we had at least twenty local young people packed into her for a fun outing at the ravine. People were sitting on knees, three deep in the backseats. There were eight more people in her than she was meant to carry. To say she was "crammed" would be putting it lightly.

We were zooming down a one-lane highway toward our destination. As you'd imagine from a group of teens squeezed into a small space, there was much laughter and hilarity. Suddenly, a policeman stepped out into the middle of the road and waved us down. We were used to the bullying tactics of the police. We expected the usual threats of arrest until the requisite bribes were secured. We were sure we would get a costly ticket, and maybe they would even detain Murray for having so many people in the car.

Murray rolled down his window. The policeman asked us where we were heading. Were we by chance going anywhere near the town of Alba Iulia?

"Well yes we are," answered "Murray the Calm." The policeman turned and signaled to another man who had just popped his head out from behind some bushes.

"Can you please take my brother there?" he asked. "He needs to get to Alba Iulia right away for urgent business."

"Of course," said Murray without blinking. "Please hop right in."

The whole thing seemed fishy, but we weren't asking questions. We were delighted Murray was not heading to jail and that we still had all our money in our pockets. Happily, we all scooted over and our load went from a mere twenty to twenty-one people. We pulled out into traffic and kept heading to our destination with a stop en route in Alba Iulia!

Only in Romania, I thought.

• • •

We did not have a landline phone. It took years on a waiting list to get one. If people wanted to tell you anything, they usually just dropped by your house. This often resulted in a social visit lasting at least a couple of hours. I gradually adjusted my mindset and chose to enjoy this cultural difference when it occurred, rather than view it as an interruption in my day "Going with the flow" kept you from "going over the edge."

One day, school was interrupted by a visit from our friendly granny, Marta. After an hour or two, the reason for her visit slowly came out. She asked if we would take some essential supplies to some friends in an extremely remote location in the mountains. Although her family owned a car, the journey was over some rough terrain and a rugged vehicle was required. Their Dacia would not be suitable. She suggested that since it was a bit of a drive, and because it was such a lovely time of year, perhaps our family would enjoy a little getaway and an overnight stay. She said she would love to take her grandchildren too, as they never got away for holidays. What's more, it was spring and the display of wildflowers in the mountains would be spectacular.

"So what do you think about the idea of taking a little weekend getaway with my family?" This query was accompanied by a soft low-pitched whistle as air rushed through the gaps in her teeth. She had been leading up to the question for the past half hour.

"The accommodations are very basic," she chirped with a jovial smile on her wrinkled face. "I hope they will be okay for you."

"Of course," I replied quite nonchalantly.

A weekend getaway. Something so simple. Something we took for granted. It hadn't dawned on me that a simple weekend getaway was quite out of reach for many Romanians.

We were always happy to help, and we knew that a request from Marta and her husband, Ion, indicated that help was truly needed. They were good, kindhearted people we really trusted. I did so love nature and seeing different parts of this spectacular country. We were definitely up for a weekend trip. It would be fun.

We made plans to make the visit in a couple of weeks.

When the weekend of the trip finally arrived, we packed a little overnight bag and headed over to the Muresan's home. As we pulled up to the house, we noticed a mountain of supplies sitting on their porch. This included an enormous sawblade about four feet in diameter, sacks of bread, all manner of tools, and other puzzling contraptions.

Yikes. What an overwhelming load of stuff to get into Candy. I flashed an assortment of eye signals at Murray, who was serenely surveying the scene.

Unperturbed, Murray set to with his expert packing skills. Apart from the massive pile of paraphernalia on the porch, the entire Muresan clan (grandparents Marta and Ion, their son and his wife and their four children) also needed to squeeze into Candy. It was definitely going to be squashed.

An hour later, Murray had done it. Astonishingly, he found a way to fit in all the gear, still leaving room for the twelve of us to squeeze into the car. He may have been able to shoehorn one more crust of bread into Candy, but that was debatable. Why the heck did we need to take that much bread anyway? Never mind. Murray had prevailed against the odds. It was an excruciatingly tight fit, but my highly talented husband had done it once again.

He slowly eased Candy out of the driveway, and we set off on our eagerly anticipated journey. Before we reached the end of their street, Ion, who never ceased smiling, leaned over to Murray. His silver front teeth glistened as he mentioned for the very first time that we needed to stop and pick up two other people who were coming with us!

Was this a joke? OMG, he was dead serious! Had it not entered his mind to mention this a couple of hours ago? My exceptionally laidback husband didn't even miss a beat. He took it all in stride and said, "Why of course! Where do they live?" I let out an inadequately masked gasp.

Five minutes later, we arrived at his friend's house. It took Murray an hour to unpack pretty much everything except the sawblade. Another hour of deep discussion ensued among the menfolk to determine which items were absolutely essential to the trip. I couldn't believe this was taking so long. It crossed my mind that an outsider might conclude these men were from the UN, making crucial planetwide life-changing decisions. Such was the intensity of their discussion over the freaking packing of Candy.

Take a breath, Leanne, I said to myself. I let the incantation swirl through my aggravated mind. *It really doesn't matter that we started our journey about four hours ago and have only gone seven miles. Big picture, Leanne . . . helping people. Leanne . . . breathe.*

This self-soothing mantra helped to calm my mind a little.

Eventually, we concertinaed back into Candy, filling every square inch of her. This time we had more people but less stuff. The girls and I were in the very back with the other little children and a couple of the younger adults. Suddenly, my girls started laughing uncontrollably. They were rolling around in absolute hysterics. I asked them what was so funny, and they pointed to the old gent sitting in front of us. He was a relative of the mountain folk we were going to stay with. We had never met him before. My eyes followed their pointing fingers. In a jiffy, I realized their unsuppressed mirth was due to the magnificently long, black curly hair protruding a couple inches out of his ears. It was really quite spectacular. I had never seen anything quite like it. I had been so busy with the repacking ordeal of the past hour that I had not even noticed this wonderfully odd phenomenon right in front of my eyes. Despite the fact I was trying in vain to tell the girls it was rude to laugh at people, they roared with full abandon at the scene just inches away.

In truth, our entire situation would be delightful fodder for a comedy show.

The combination of curly black ear hair, fourteen people jammed into Candy, gobs of who knows what stuffed in around us, the unsavory odors of infrequently washed bodies, strong garlic and onion breath, the bumpy mountain road, and the sweltering hot summer's day provided more than enough storylines for an entire season of sitcom humor. This was downright hilarious! My girls had got it right. Forget the rules. I joined them in their unfettered delight and roared with uninhibited laughter too.

The comedic aspect, however, was about to dissipate. We really were going to a remote mountain place. Roads deteriorated into dirt tracks. At times we drove along riverbeds. It was a really tortuous route, and in the heat our laughter soon subsided as motion sickness kicked in. Candy did not come equipped with air-conditioning because cooling a vehicle in Scotland was beyond ridiculous.

We had learned that many of the people in villages and small towns like Aiud subscribed to a list of unusual beliefs. We were about to discover yet another one. Some of our passengers believed that wind flow from a window would cause ear infections, so car windows had to be kept tightly shut while in motion. I understood that you might be overly cautious when you have limited access to medicine, but good gracious it was in the nineties outside and there were fourteen of us packed in tight. We were rocking around in a tin can. There was no way we were going to keep the windows closed, regardless of the increasing protests about life-threatening drafts from Marta. Once we started bouncing along rocky riverbeds, threatening to dislodge our loose fillings, nausea began to set in. Politeness headed for the exit.

"Open the damn windows!" I yelled before I could check my emotions. "We will all faint in the heat back here."

Four windows rolled down in unison and utter silence filled the car. Our friends had just experienced a she-wolf coming to life. Seconds later, Marta magically whipped out four woolen hats, as if she had accessed Hermione's beaded bag bestowed with its Undetectable Extension Charm. She stuffed those hats on the roasting-hot heads of her grandchildren, tucking eight ears safely away. I was totally perplexed why one would even consider bringing woolen hats on a hot summer's day, but what did I know? Quite honestly, I was just happy the windows were open.

Up and up we climbed along a dirt trail. We were miles from civilization. I was fascinated by how people survived out here in this beautiful remote wilderness. We had not seen any sign of human life for ages.

Murray pulled Candy to a sudden halt and announced we should all evacuate the vehicle. No need to tell any of us in the back to get out. In a hot second, I threw open the back door. The woolly headed kids, my girls, and I all tumbled out as best we could, given the circumstances of our containment. It was an all-out struggle to get free of the trappings. Within a nanosecond of our escape, Victoria was collecting wildflowers and Julia was covered in mud. Those were my girls. The smell of fresh air rather than garlic breath was simply glorious. Release was a sweet thing.

We had come to a fast-flowing river with a very narrow wooden "bridge" across it. In reality, it was just two planks attached to each bank. A little way up the mountain, we could see a couple of little huts in the distance. We learned from smiley Ion that this was our final destination.

Murray was having qualms about taking Candy across the planks. Now remember, this was my Canadian husband who had driven an SUV for fifty-five miles across frozen Lake Athabasca in -30°C. He was always up for a good challenge, but when he expressed reservations, I listened. He stepped out onto the bridge and jumped up and down on it. He walked across and back. He crouched down to eyeball the distance between the planks and compare it with the vehicle's wheel span. A low whistle escaped from the side of his mouth.

"Pretty tight," he said, "but I think it is doable!"

Are you freaking kidding me? was my first thought. "Okay, if you think you can do it, but please be careful," was what I actually said. I had been a grumpy killjoy for long enough and that sweet mountain air was already producing a calming effect on me.

The older adults had remained stolidly statuesque in their seats, like sardines in a can. Now Murray ordered them out of the vehicle, and we helped to pry them out of it. Once the Land Rover had been vacated, Murray was ready to cross the "bridge." Shit no! What was he doing? He was revving up the engine to a fever pitch. He had decided to gun it at top speed across the planks. I observed the tire overhang on all sides in horror, waiting for Candy to go careening off the edge and into the abyss below. But in the blink of an eye, Candy shot across to the other side of the ravine like a supersonic jet. Murray abruptly braked and jumped out of Candy with a huge grin across his adorable face.

"Made it!" he crooned with great pride. I responded via furious eye signals: "Okay, smarty-pants, but next time remind me not to watch. I can only take a limited number of heart-stopping events in one lifetime."

The old people piled back into Candy, but the kids and I would have none of it. We were all happy to walk the rest of the way. I noticed with pure joy that not a single woolen hat was on any little head. Those silly hats had miraculously disapparated as quickly as they had appeared. We ambled up the stunning hillside toward our evening abode, happy to have finally arrived.

• • •

"Simple," as Marta had put it, was definitely an understatement. Even though the house we had arrived at was fairly clean, "hut" was probably more of an apt description. It was really just a large room with a wood stove, a table, a couple of chairs, and a very suspect-looking bed with a straw mattress. The floors were dirt, covered with simple planks. There was no running water. They had a well outside and filled buckets with water when necessary. I realized these kind people were country folk in every sense of the word. I felt as though I had stepped back in time. At that very moment, I imagined I was on the set of Fiddler on the Roof and Tevye would break into song with "Matchmaker."

Our hosts' gratitude was off the charts when they saw the massive amounts of supplies literally bursting from the vehicle. My golly, how in the world did we fit all that stuff and fourteen people into Candy? I was married to a genius who should have been designing spaces for the Container Store.

Candy was a complete enigma to these folks. They had never seen anything like her. Their single mode of transportation was horse and cart. They sat in her and inspected everything with huge smiles. When Murray asked if they would like a ride, you would have thought they had just won the Powerball jackpot. "Don't cross the bridge!" I said in what I thought was a whisper but came out more like a strangled screech. Several of the adults shot me startled glances. *Okay, Leanne . . . chill . . . enjoy the beauty all around.* It really was jaw-dropping scenery, and thankfully my motion sickness was subsiding.

The supplies we brought included copious amounts of delicious food that Marta and her daughter-in-law had prepared. Interestingly, I noticed that our hosts only ate the fresh bread that had been bought from the bakery that morning. They devoured it. It dawned on me that they grew and made pretty much everything they ate. The fresh bakery-made bread was a luxury for them. Only then did I fully understand why we had schlepped so much bread with us. Boring old bread was an exciting gift for these enchanting and somewhat toothless people. Once again I thought, *Yes, it's all relative isn't it?* We take so much for granted in our richly blessed lives.

"Mummy, I need the bathroom," Julia said as she tugged on my sleeve.

Now that was a thought. "Where is the bathroom?" I asked our guests. They pointed toward the barn a little way up the hill. I was handed a few pages of newsprint from a very old book and some ancient-looking handwritten letters. Oh boy, this was the toilet paper! Yikes! We were used to Romanian toilet paper that came embedded with small wood chips (no kidding), but this was something entirely different. What were we in for?

The barn sat on a hillside. As instructed, we headed around to the far side of the barn on the steepest slope. With much trepidation, we set out on our search.

I had seen a lot of really nasty bathrooms in Romania, but I was having a particularly uneasy feeling about this one. We rounded the corner of the barn, and there it was at the top of a few rickety steps. We gingerly climbed the stairs, and because I did not want to touch anything, I delicately kicked open the door. Something made from a few rough planks of wood nailed together around an opening faced us. It was the most rudimentary commode I could have ever imagined. For a moment, I had a memory of my childhood family camping trips and Dad's bright-blue and cherry-red La-La's. But there was no resemblance when I really thought about it. Compared to this, La-La's was pure opulence and luxury.

As you'd guess, the smell was pretty putrid. Suddenly, something worse than the horrific stench caught my attention. I looked down through the slats that formed the floor of the "room" we were in. Was that movement below us? What was that noise underneath us? Dusk was approaching, and the light was fading. It was hard to determine the source of the movement. I peered harder as my eyes adjusted to the relative darkness of the room. To my horror, I saw a couple of excited-looking grunting pigs trampling around in shit just a few feet below us. I almost fainted when I realized that the waste that entered the toilet dropped directly below to the pigs. They were eagerly waiting to gobble up everything. Bile bubbled up into my throat, and I whirled a stunned

Julia around with spectacular dexterity, turned on my heels, and we skedaddled down the steps.

"Let's use the woods tonight, darling. I think that will be fun!"

I gagged three more times as we zeroed in on the closest tree. It was definitely time for my family to go on water rations for the rest of this trip. There was no way in hell we were using a toilet with pigs running around underneath it. I had my limits, and I had just hit them.

This remote location had no electricity, so everyone went to bed when it got dark. We were told that the women and children were sleeping in the house. The men were sleeping over at the barn, in the hayloft above the cows. No freaking way. As there was only one barn, that meant they were also sleeping above the pigs. I gagged again.

Thankful to be female at that moment, I bid Murray adieu and headed back into the house with the girls. I mentioned he ought to find some nose plugs. Even Mr. Calm looked a little apprehensive about this turn of events. His unease was amplified when I revealed, via surreptitious whisper, the scandalous details of our bathroom expedition.

As honored guests, the girls and I were kindly given the straw mattress bed. Visions of bedbugs raced through my mind. I protested vociferously, insisting that I would not even think of taking their bed. Our kind hosts would have none of it. So the girls and I crawled onto the sagging mattress, and everyone else lay on blankets on the floor. They were soundly asleep in a jiffy. I have always been an annoyingly light sleeper and tend to need optimal sleeping conditions to ensure I get a good night's rest. An old, sagging, lumpy straw mattress in a room full of snoring women and children did not fall into the "optimal" category. As I lay there, my mind whirled. Today had been quite an adventure. I suspected I probably would never have another day like it for the rest of my life. As I pondered this, I was filled with a deep gratitude for the many blessings I had.

I was appreciative of these experiences, no matter how far outside my comfort zone they took me. I was thankful to be able to make a little difference in a few people's lives over the course of my journey.

• • •

I believe that a single act of generosity expands far beyond its initial intent. We may not even be aware of the knock-on effect that it engenders. One kind action can set in motion changes that will continue to reverberate throughout eternity. It's a universal law that we can't deny.

Our aid projects thrived over the next couple of years in Aiud. We helped many people in the community and helped change lives for the better, one little act at a time. Donations from abroad flowed in to support our work and enabled us to continue distributing much needed aid. We also obtained a couple of scholarships for young people to study in the UK, offering them the chance of a lifetime. The new medical clinic was open, and Dr. Becky oversaw operations providing affordable, top quality health care. It was so rewarding to see our efforts making a tangible difference.

CHAPTER 13

· · · · · · · · · · · · · · · · · ·

Survival 101 and Crispy Skin Strips

O ver the next couple of years, we became involved with the larger expat community in Cluj-Napoca, a city forty miles to the north of Aiud. At the time, Cluj had a population of 300,000. After Bucharest, Cluj was the second largest city in Romania and the center of a tremendous amount of aid, commerce, and new development projects. People from all over the Western world who were working with nongovernmental organizations, embassies, private companies, the Babes-Bolyai University, and within government organizations made up this expat community. Here we found a group of likeminded people who had come to Romania to bring aid, resources, and skills to help rebuild this nation. Networking with many of these dedicated and brilliant people was essential for our work and morale. We needed one another and collectively worked to support our surrounding community. The camaraderie and support among this expat group was invaluable.

One day while we were in Cluj visiting another nonprofit to coordinate some resources, we met an American family in the process of moving back to the States. They mentioned they were renting a house from an older Romanian couple who lived in the basement. They told us it was a great living arrangement, the landlords were wonderful, and it was in an excellent location. They wondered if we knew anyone who might be interested in taking over their lease.

A few days prior, we had received the unwelcome news that the owner of our current house in Aiud was thinking of selling. Our landlord informed us that we might need to relocate at fairly short notice. This disclosure had sent me into a bit of an internal tailspin. The thought of being homeless disturbed me. I experienced horror flashbacks of the chicken-murderer's junkhole and the Speckles debacle. I shuddered, then took a few deep breaths to remind myself that if one door closes, another most certainly would open. I focused on our amazing track record. So I quieted my anxiety and reinforced my hope that something wonderful would appear.

A little quivery buzz welled up inside of me when we unexpectedly heard about the rental possibility in Cluj. I turned and quietly said to Murray, "Maybe we should consider moving to live in Cluj?" It was no surprise that he was thinking the same thing. Immediately, we made an appointment to look at the house and meet the owners.

A couple of hours later, we sat outside under the grapevines in the garden of their home. As we sipped on homemade wine, ate cherries from their garden, and chatted with them, we knew we had come home. The girls were skipping around the yard, visiting the chickens and pigs in their pens, picking fruit from trees, making daisy chains, and cuddling kittens. They were already calling the owners *Buni* and *Bunicuţ*, the Romanian words for granny and grandpa.

Two weeks later, we moved to Cluj and into our new residence.

Compared to prior living situations, this house was like a palace. It was on a paved street and was gated behind a high wall for security purposes. It had a telephone and even a television with several channels, including the BBC and Bloomberg. Even though we had always been avid listeners of the BBC World Service on the radio, we felt like we were finally back in touch with the outside world.

The owners, Ion and Iliana, had a son who had immigrated to Canada. When he left home, they had moved downstairs into the basement. We rented the entire upstairs, which had three bedrooms, a bathroom, and a large great room that doubled up as a schoolroom, dining room, and living room. The only thing missing was a kitchen, but fortunately we had the use of a small kitchen downstairs. Running up and down twenty narrow little stairs with all our food and dishes on trays was just a little inconvenient, but in the big picture, it was far superior to our previous arrangements.

Ion and Iliana loved the girls and treated them like their own grandchildren. It didn't take us long to teach Iliana to stop pinching the girls' fresh pink cheeks. They had a huge backyard garden with many fruit trees. They kindly shared their produce and fruit. They had a chicken house full of laying hens and a pigpen that always had a couple of residents being fattened up for slaughter. There were numerous outdoor cats to keep the mice at bay and a dog that depressingly remained tied up all day. The dog's sole purpose was to bark at any would-be intruders. Pigs were more prized than dogs, because they were a food source.

A bakery was located right next door to our new home, and we awoke daily to the delectable aroma of freshly baked bread wafting past our windows. Every morning, the girls ran next door for a loaf of bread—their first chore of the day. Some days the bread was almost too hot to carry, so they ran back to the house juggling the steaming hot, round loaf to stop their little hands from burning. Inevitably, the bread arrived back in the kitchen with a couple of little finger-sized chunks missing. Who could blame them? Who can resist fresh warm bread?

We established an efficient new routine for the girls' schooling. They promptly started at eight a.m. with piano lessons and classes. We'd complete their schoolwork by lunchtime with no trouble at all. That left the afternoons and evenings free for us to work and for the girls to play. Right after lunch, they headed out to the street to play with newfound friends, who had also finished school by early afternoon.

Most Romanian children had very few toys and became masters of creating games with such simple things as sticks and stones. The girls spent hours out on the streets with their friends making huts and forts. They devised remarkably creative stories with many twists and turns. Every evening they would come in for dinner absolutely filthy. Their very white skin had turned a gritty shade of grey from their outdoor adventures. I was immensely grateful to turn on the bathtub faucet and get steaming hot water on demand. No more boiling water in pots and carrying them to the bathtub. Life was definitely becoming easier.

• • •

Over the course of the next couple of years, our schedule became so much fuller. We organized and hosted numerous volunteer teams working on projects in Cluj and Aiud. People of all nationalities and backgrounds joined us. We secured accommodations for our volunteers in a new hostel that had opened up in Cluj. It had several rooms with bunk beds and working bathrooms. At the time, it felt as though we were offering our teams five-star accommodations, but in reality it was very basic.

There were still very few restaurants, so most of the time I was the chef and our home was the restaurant. Despite the fact that living was easier and there were more resources available in Cluj, it still took a lot of time to source and organize meals for large teams of people and we soon realized that we needed help. The additional roles of schoolteacher and Mum meant that life was pretty full for me. I became the master of multitasking.

We put out the word that we needed some help. Gill, a lovely young woman from Scotland, eventually joined us as a nanny. She supervised all the school lessons and was a wonderful asset to our family. I hired local women to help with food prep, cleaning, running errands, and so on. I was so thankful for all this help because it allowed the wheels of our organization to turn more smoothly. Well, as smoothly as things could in early post-Communist Romania.

New little "supermarkets" popped up here and there. The supply of food items for purchase was increasing. We still couldn't just help ourselves to items off the shelves. Instead, we asked the clerk behind the counter to pass the food to us and then added it to our mini-shopping carts. Security gates prevented us from exiting the shop until we paid for our goods. It was a rather weird way to shop for groceries, but we didn't complain because we were finally purchasing food with a lot less difficulty.

A few restaurants began to open. It was always a tad comical to take guests to some of these establishments. On our arrival, the erstwhile waiter would pass us beautiful leather-bound menus. They contained an exhaustive list of dining options, often written in English. Now when I say exhaustive, think Cheesecake Factory menu on steroids! Our guests would look in awe at the impressive tome they held. Slowly they'd scroll through it, overwhelmed by all the astonishing choices and culinary delights. The waiter would come back to take our order. Our guests would attempt to place several orders, only to be told the particular dish they sought was not available that day. When the stoic waiter was finally asked, "What do you have available today?" he would whip out a single sheet, hand it to us, and say with great pride, "Today we have pork!"

"Right then, pork it shall be!"

• • •

Speaking of pork . . . on the first weekend of each December, with the Christmas season imminent, fattened pigs would be on the verge of fulfilling their destiny. There were no presidential pardons for these good fellows.

We awoke at the crack of dawn one Saturday morning to the unnerving sound of blood-curdling screaming that reverberated throughout the neighborhood. The sound was intense, horrific, terrible, chilling. We had never heard anything like it before. Goosebumps exploded all over our bodies, and Murray and I flew out of bed. We tripped over each other to get outside to inspect the commotion.

On our driveway stood Ion, Iliana, and a group of gnarly looking people bundled up in thick winter coats and hats. They had just slit the throat of one of the pigs that mere moments ago had been happily grunting around in his pen. His pen mate, by contrast, was still very much alive, watching the whole thing and screaming like a banshee. Rivulets of blood were gushing down the driveway and running out under the gate and onto the street. As we surveyed this truly macabre scene, we noted that we could hear the same sounds ringing out all around the neighborhood. Pigs were being slaughtered up and down the street.

Iliana bounced up to us and eagerly explained that this was the traditional day for slaughtering pigs to ensure a sufficient supply of food for the holiday festivities. The second howling pig was soon to follow the fate of his luckless pen mate. Relatives would soon bring their doomed pigs over to the house to face their maker as well. It was a group effort that would span much of the day. An early start was essential.

As I surveyed the motley, bloodied group of men and women standing around the pig's limp torso, I discerned that there was a positively festive feel in the air. It was quite the scene. And then it hit me—the girls!!

With my nightie flying through the crisp morning air, I hoofed it back into the house as if I were on fire. I got there just in the nick of time. Two sleepy little figures in their PJs were rambling barefoot down the hallway toward the front door. In a hot second, I twirled them around and marched them right back into the living room. I threw *The Sound of Music* video into the video player, turned the TV on as loudly as possible, and told the girls not to go outside or look out the window. It was a morning to stay inside and enjoy videos! I was going to cook delicious pancakes, and we would have a big, fun Saturday morning breakfast feast!

Well, of course, the girls weren't to be fooled. They had also heard the horrific screams and wanted to know what was happening. Upon hearing the general details, Victoria turned a paler shade of white and got a bit wobbly on her feet. I so wished I could whisk her away from the gruesome scene outside her bedroom window. But there was no escaping. It was already well underway, and to leave the property we'd have to walk right past the site of the porcine massacre.

Murray and the girls were cuddled up to watch TV, so I headed down to the kitchen to prepare the promised pancake feast. Although I could still hear the sounds from all over the neighborhood, the decibel level in our yard had, thankfully, markedly decreased.

A few moments later, I heard a loud hissing. What in the world was going on now? I am not a terribly queasy person—after all, my physiotherapy training had included a year of human dissection— but I am a somewhat inquisitive person. I decided that I really had to throw caution to the wind, venture outside, and investigate the latest developments in the killing fields. To be honest, this whole event was somehow weirdly fascinating. I had front row seats to "Survival Skills 101."

I put the pancakes on hold and boldly stepped out the door. Right in front of me a man wielded a blowtorch, spewing flames all over the now-departed pig. What a ghastly smell! He was burning the hair off the pig's body. The skin was turning a very crispy black color. Wow, this was unwholesomely interesting and for a moment all pancake thoughts vanished from my mind.

Suddenly, and horrifyingly, Ion whisked out a very sharp knife and sliced off the pig's ears, tail, and some long slices of crispy charred skin. His gang of compatriots egged him on with unbridled cheering. Holy moly! What the heck? He then handed these prized morsels to several lucky recipients. My stomach turned as I watched them eagerly devour these parts that had been on the pig just a few seconds ago. I guess this was breakfast. I noticed that țuică had already started flowing. Smiles were spreading and laughter escalated in our backyard abattoir. My stomach turned. Maybe I wasn't as tough as I thought. Suddenly, pancakes and coffee seemed like such a deliciously simple dining experience compared to pig's ears, tail, and skin strips accompanied by țuică. I scurried right back to the kitchen.

Later, Iliana told me they wouldn't waste a thing. They used every single part of the pig. Eww. My mind rebelled against that thought. Several days later, the girls and I had an impromptu lesson from Iliana on how to make soap. We went outside at the end of school lessons and found Iliana standing over a big pot of bubbling goo. She informed us that it was soap production day. The girls got very involved in the activity. It was a lot of fun and definitely more interesting than math class. I didn't have the heart to tell them that the main ingredient was fat from their favorite pig. I swore Iliana to secrecy. Soap making seemed sufficiently divorced from pig's fat, and in this case I figured ignorance was bliss. I did, however, make a definitive decision to stick with Dove.

Anyway, back to my backyard. Butchering took several hours and as the day progressed, it started snowing and everything outside began to freeze. Evening bonfires glowed as parties popped up all around the neighborhood. The weary butchers roasted their fresh pink meat while they consumed alarming quantities of alcoholic beverage. Everyone kicked back, relaxed, and enjoyed a hearty feast after a long day of slaughtering.

This marked the end of our all-day self-imposed incarceration. Done with watching endless videos and playing board games, we decided it was safe to venture outside for an evening walk in the snow and some much needed fresh air. We pulled on heavy jackets, snow boots, scarves, and mitts and left our confinement for a tromp in the snow. The peace and quiet of newly fallen snow was magical, especially after the earlier cacophony and commotion. We pelted each other with snowballs as we walked down deserted streets. Almost all evidence of the day's horrors were gone. We did, however, notice pink stains in the snow peeking out from under all the gates we walked past in our neighborhood, a reminder that life in Romania was still far from easy for most people.

It was good to remember how fortunate we were. By Western living standards, Murray and I were living fairly frugally. Compared to most of the world, we were extremely rich. We always had food to eat and never wondered how we would be able to feed our children. That was not the case with many of our neighbors.

That night, I pondered again why we as a human race seem to find it so easy to complain about the things we believe we lack in life. In truth, we have so much to be thankful for and to rejoice about. It is indeed curious.

CHAPTER 14

. . . .

A Cornfield and
a Whole Lot of Grit

I don't remember exactly how we met Dan and Simona Baciu, but I am forever grateful that I know these two truly amazing human beings. Dan is a medical doctor, and Simona is a teacher. In lots of ways we were kindred spirits. Dan and Simona loved life and people. Despite enduring extreme hardship in days past, they maintained a positive and beautiful outlook on life. They were pure gold.

They loved their country. Now that the old regime had fallen, they were hungry for positive change. The education system, among other areas, required an overhaul. Many Romanians were very well educated, but teaching techniques were rigid and punitive. It was difficult to overturn decades of firmly entrenched systems, and change did not happen overnight, especially when resources were scarce.

Simona wanted to implement teaching methods whereby children were taught with love and kindness and encouraged to be creative and independent. This approach was vastly different from the current system that primarily used fear as a teaching tool. She believed that "every child should have the chance to achieve excellence by highlighting their individual qualities and by forming independent, responsible, self-confident individuals who could make a positive difference in the world." It was a radical idea and departed from traditional education in Romania at that time. Simona wanted to open a preschool/kindergarten that would use Western teaching methods incorporating the values she believed in. Nothing like it existed in the country. The wheels of private enterprise were very slowly beginning to churn, but this did not extend to the educational realm in any way, shape, or form.

Every time they shared their ideas with us, my *inner voice* yelled, "Yes, yes, yes! Get involved." So we did. We had completed a lot of projects up to this point in our journey, but there was something very special about this partnership. We felt as though supporting Dan and Simona was the very reason we had come to Romania.

To many, it may sound simple to start a preschool, but believe me, this was no easy task in post-Communist Romania. A dizzying number of obstacles sat in the way. First off, Simona was a high school teacher in a state school, so she would have to leave her secure job and income. Dan and Simona didn't have any savings, and their family income would be halved. Like most Romanians in post-Communist Romania, they were already struggling to make ends meet each week.

Without any resources, it was impossible to rent a place for the new school. There was always an inordinate amount of red tape and every government agency wanted a cut of the pie in any new project. A preschool would be no exception. I cannot begin to explain the amount of bureaucracy and bribery involved. It often took days of waiting in lines just to obtain a single approval stamp for even minor things. If you could get past these obstacles, there was still the question of purchasing equipment and materials for the school. Remember, most of the shops were empty. There was no Amazon. The doors to the outside world were only just beginning to open. We'd have to source almost everything from outside of the country. And importing goods created even more bureaucracy.

Next, the preschool needed teachers, and those teachers would have to be trained in the new teaching methods. Naturally, they had to be paid a living wage.

Finally, this new school would need students. No one paid for private education in Romania. It was unheard of. The prevailing mindset was that education was the responsibility of the state. In addition, people just did not have the resources to pay for it. Most people were reeling from a dire lack of everyday resources, so spending money on a child's education, no matter how wonderful it might be, was considered ridiculous. Even though Simona planned to offer hardship scholarships, she would need paying students to support the school. None of this would be subsidized by the state, that was a given.

Absolutely none of these obstacles deterred Dan and Simona one iota. They were going to make it happen, somehow and someway.

In 1993, Simona quit her paid teaching job and opened Happy Kids Kindergarten in a tiny room of their small home. Until now, they had rented this room to a young man for extra income. The loss of this rental income was another significant hit to their finances, but they were not deterred even though they had no other resources to draw on.

The first class began with twelve children, ages two to six. We promoted it as an alternative to the dull and punitive learning experience of the state education system. It was inspired by an international curriculum, using modern teaching methods and innovative approaches to learning. Simona was the only teacher. Within a year, the number of students in the preschool grew to twenty. But all of this was not without cost to Dan and Simona. Since their regular income had been cut by more than half, there were many days they had no money for food. Most days their children ate at their grandma's home.

Dan and Simona were big thinkers, always looking for ways to help children in situations where resources were lacking the most. In 1994, they started their first community service program, supporting a kindergarten for deaf students. They also organized a playgroup for children in orphanages.

By 1995, the kindergarten had outgrown the founders' house, and they decided to rent a one-room apartment in the neighborhood. The number of students immediately jumped to thirty-two. The apartment quickly became cramped. It lacked an outside play area for the children, so they decided to look for something even bigger.

In 1996, they found a small house with a couple of good-sized rooms and a small yard that would be a perfect new home for the Happy Kids Kindergarten. In no time we completed renovations with the assistance of a couple of our volunteer teams. Simona then recruited three likeminded teachers she had worked with previously and trained them in new teaching methods. The school grew to forty-five students, ages two to six. That same year, Dan and Simona officially founded the Happy Kids Foundation with a mission to provide education with international standards of excellence for children ages one to eighteen.

Next, we established the first afterschool program in Cluj. It was a real hit. Among other activities, we offered English lessons for elementary-school-aged students, taught by our volunteers. We organized the first parenting program in Cluj, a new concept for Romanians. The classes were always overbooked. Parenting practices that we considered normal were frequently mind-blowing to Romanians. For example, fathers were seldom involved in raising children. Traditionally, it was a woman's domain. We offered examples of how fathers could be more involved in family life. I am told that some of the parenting ideas we taught in those classes changed the face of family life forever.

By 1997, the number of children attending the Happy Kids Kindergarten had grown to sixty, swamping the small two-room house. Fortunately, they were able to rent a third room in an adjacent building. They now had three teachers and three assistant teachers. It was the first school to embrace the concept of "assistant teacher" in Romania.

Once again, Happy Kids outgrew its space, and now the founders were thinking about a permanent location for their school. We started to look for a small piece of land with Dan and Simona. One day, Simona called over to our house, bubbling with excitement. She thought she had found the perfect place for the school. We piled into Candy and took off to explore Simona's find. She had discovered a narrow cornfield tucked away not far from the city center. It did indeed look like it would be the perfect location for a new school. The property was behind a high wall, but the gate would not open. As we wandered around the outside, the neighbors came out and suggested we scale the wall. Up and over we went. As we walked around, we just knew this was where we would build the Happy Kids School. Now we had to find the means to purchase the land and build a school.

On a visit back to Scotland, I shared Dan and Simona's story with everyone I met. I looked for help at every turn. Happy Kids desperately needed financial backing. One day we visited with our friends the Scotts, who had so generously donated the Land Rover for our work. We told them all about Dan and Simona and their huge vision to change the education system in Romania. The Scotts expressed an interest in making a trip to Romania to see this firsthand.

This was an unquestionably exciting development, mostly because there is nothing like a cross-cultural experience to open your heart and mind to the possibility of involvement. The Scotts were the most generous of human beings, with resources to give to worthy philanthropic ventures. Without a doubt, Happy Kids School fit into the "worthy philanthropic venture" category. It was no surprise that the Scotts became involved in the Happy Kids Foundation after meeting with Dan and Simona. They provided the funds to purchase the land and build a new school on the cornfield. Over the next few years, they gave not only much needed financial support but also tremendous educational support to turn this fantastic vision into something far greater than just a preschool.

• • •

Over the next few years, the school grew in numbers and reputation.

In February 1999, after we were no longer living in Romania, I had the delightful pleasure of returning to Cluj for a visit. Lucinda Scott and I were honored guests for the opening of their new school, located on the aforementioned cornfield. Happy Kids Kindergarten now boasted six classrooms, a library, a gym, and a small playground.

A series of small steps led to this school being built. The first baby step was to open a small preschool class in a tiny room in Dan and Simona's home. This was followed by many subsequent little steps, until finally in 2000, the kindergarten had a staggering one hundred sixty students.

Now they were ready to open the Happy Kids International Primary School. Guided by the principles they used for the kindergarten, the primary (elementary) school was the first in Romania to use an international curriculum. In the same manner as the kindergarten, the Happy Kids Primary School started with twelve students.

Happy Kids kindergarten which began in Simona's home in 1993, is now Transylvania College, a world-class educational facility offering the Cambridge International Curriculum in a unique multicultural environment for children aged two to eighteen. The children, teachers, and staff represent twenty-five nations from six continents. Thousands of Romanian children have now been educated at this exceptional school. Many of the students are from underprivileged backgrounds and receive scholarships. In September 2013, the school opened the only boarding facility in the country. The Transylvania College Boarding House offers placement for boys and girls ages thirteen years old and higher. The school's track record of excellence includes a long list of national and international awards.

Over the last twenty years, Dan and Simona have been instrumental in rewriting the Romanian education syllabus, helping to bring change to the state education system. Simona sent me a message a few months back that I am proud to share.

> *Dear Leanne,*
> *I am so excited to get news from you.*
> *We just got home from Sinaia, where it was one of the most honoring experiences I ever had. The Princess Margarita of Romania decorated me for the outstanding school we have and for the support and development we brought in the Romanian National Education. You were with us. We thought of you and Murray and how we could never be here without your friendship, which helped us to follow our dream. God is the One we have to thank for bringing you into our life forever. God bless you dear friend,*
>
> *Lots of love,*
> *Simona*

Their vision for change started as something so tiny and seemingly impossible, yet it grew to something truly magnificent. They believed in the *power of things unseen* and did what they knew they needed to do, no matter how farfetched it seemed. They followed that voice inside of themselves and changed an entire nation's education system. In my eyes, they are true heroes.

• • •

I naturally possess fairly good communication skills. Understanding people and talking with them comes reasonably easy to me. My friends call it my genius. This natural gift of communication makes me a great networker. This was an extremely useful skill for our work in Romania. Looking back, I can see that one of our primary roles while living there was networking. We connected people and resources from outside of the country with those who had specific needs within Romania. If we had not lived in Romania, our networking would not have been so effective. We would not have accomplished all that we were able to. I am sure we would never have met Dan and Simona, as I know we would never have begun working in Cluj.

We have always followed our *inner voice*. It led us to relocate to Europe when our girls were babies, even when we had limited resources. It was an incredibly difficult move. At times we wondered why we were there. But in Scotland we got the opportunity to join a volunteer team visiting Romania. This eventually opened a door for us to move there. Subsequently, we met the Scotts and later connected them with Dan and Simona. Transylvania College exists because of that one connection. To this day, the college creates unbelievable opportunities for Romanian children.

If we had not taken all of our small steps, we would have missed out on the sense of fulfillment that we now possess, a sense of having played a small part in changing a nation for the better. I cannot begin to describe how internally rich I feel simply because we jumped into the unknown and followed what we knew we were meant to do.

For more information on Transylvania College today, go to http://transylvania-college.ro

CHAPTER 15

· · · · · · · · · · · · · · · · · · ·

Lip Gloss and a Room
with a View

I love having fun. Taking vacations and time away from a busy schedule is essential to maintaining sanity. There is something about laughter and fun that brings a new perspective and freshness to your outlook on life. It chases away your woes and worries. While living in Romania, we worked hard and a lot of the time our living conditions were far from easy. It was crucial to get away and kick up our heels, even if it was just for a day. I always returned home feeling like my brain had rebooted. I had a clearer picture of everything.

We loved visiting Dan and Simona's rustic cabin in the small mountain town of Baisoara. Our two families would often pack up and head to the mountains. In winter it was magical. Fluffy powder snow made the whole area breathtakingly beautiful. We took many spectacular treks through the forest, tromping through snow up to our knees, laughing and talking incessantly. Simona and I are two peas in a pod, and the two of us would jabber on, hardly allowing our two gentle-spirited husbands a word in! Every time we visited the cabin, we consumed copious amounts of delicious homecooked food. Once it got dark, we fell asleep wrapped in thick sleeping bags to stave off the cold.

In the summer, we hiked spectacular mountain trails and sat around the outdoor campfire roasting sausages and imbibing delicious Romanian wine. Frequently, we dozed off reading books, soporific from the fresh mountain air. The stars in the clear night sky were spectacular. Initially, there was no power or running water at the cabin. None of that mattered, because we felt like we were in heaven on earth.

We often took our volunteer teams for daytrips to the cabin. We hoped they would leave Romania having received as much as they had given, and this seemed to be the perfect place for receiving. Before long, we began running weekend retreats not only for our volunteers, but also for local Romanians. Life was still hard for many. Our retreats were a new idea, a time to breathe. The Romanians loved them, and the camps were always full.

Dan and Simona continued running retreats at their cabin after we left Romania. In 2011, after years of hosting summer camps, Dan established "Village on the Hill." He transformed their simple cabin into a beautiful resort camp. He relocated several one-hundred-year-old traditional houses to the site and modernized them. Today, large summer camps and retreats continue to run at this venue. It is a spectacular environment for teachers and students to learn about leadership, mindfulness, and socioemotional well-being. This amazing work continues today, enriching the lives of many from all over the world.

Murray and I are delighted that once again we have the opportunity to assist with these camps.

For more information on Village on the Hill Retreats go to www. simplicityretreat.com.

• • •

One of our weekend getaways was a visit with English friends living and working on a project in Timisoara. We took the train instead of making the five-hour drive from Cluj. I'm not exactly sure why we chose the train, perhaps because it was more direct and we thought it would be easier than driving. Little did we know how wrong we were.

Train travel in Romania was an experience in itself. It was the predominant means of transportation during Communist rule. The Căile Ferate Române is the state railway carrier of Romania, and it boasts the fourth largest train network in Europe. There are more than 6,700 miles of tracks crisscrossing the country. Every little town had a train station of some description. The trains were extremely long, and usually, a multitude of people waited to board them. Often at these stations there were just a few yards of platform, or more frequently, no platform at all. This meant that most people would board directly from the track at ground level. It was a thoroughly dangerous but completely accepted practice.

Trains were one of the few things that ran like clockwork. Romanians maintained great pride in the fact that trains never left the station late. The only complicating factor was that the train was frequently a little tardy in arriving. This left a minuscule window of time in which a mass of passengers had to disembark and be replaced by an equally large number of embarking passengers. It was a merciless process. The train waited for no one and would leave slow-acting passengers helplessly stranded beside the tracks as it chugged away.

Since boarding was at track level, the first step up onto the train for a person of average stature was often at waist level. Ingress and egress was an athletic feat, and certainly wasn't for the fainthearted or dimwitted. Passengers hauled themselves up to the first step and those behind them on the tracks pushed them from underneath. I was startled the first time I saw this. We always approached train travel with a little trepidation.

To ensure we all got onto the train with our luggage, we had a well-designed plan. Tall Murray would hop onto the train first. Next, I would hand the luggage up to Murray, who would squat to grab it and hoist it up into the train. The girls were conveyed onto the train in a similar manner. Finally, Murray would yank me up to join our happy little family. This usually worked well, and we pretty much had the routine down pat. Any army general would have been proud of the alacrity with which we usually executed this strategy. Once on the train, we would locate a spot as far away from the latrine as possible, because without fail, a horrific odor always emanated from this "convenience." There was no air-conditioning or heating on the trains, so in winter the smell was merely bad, but in summer the stench was atrocious. I have been "blessed" with a very acute sense of smell, which unfortunately was not an advantageous attribute while living in Romania. The smell from the train bathrooms topped the nasty charts. I was so thankful to learn a helpful trick from a friend, whereby I liberally doused my wrists with strong perfume prior to train travel. I would hold a wrist up to my nose for the entire journey. On the whole, this cunning ploy worked pretty well, diverting the sensitive membranes in my nasal passages.

On this trip to Timisoara, the train arrived into Cluj late and throngs of anxious people massed along the tracks. A general feeling of panic and confusion ensued. People were nervous they would not make it onto their carriage before departure, so there was a lot of shoving and pushing going on. We had staked out our spot beside the tracks and were holding firm despite the melee around us. We were ready to move at the speed of light to execute our well laid-out embarkation plan.

As we were only going for the weekend, we were traveling light, with just one little overnight bag that Murray had already flung over his shoulder. While the train was still screeching to a stop, Murray dashed alongside it and jumped up onto the first step with an alacrity and speed that would make any Olympic high jumper proud. I had a daughter in each hand. My little purse was strapped across my shoulder and hanging in front of my chest for safekeeping. I had no other luggage to worry about on this trip. We were pretty confident that this particular boarding would be a cinch.

We jogged down the platform toward the door where Murray had started his ascent. Suddenly, from out of nowhere, a gang of deft thieves swarmed around me and attempted to pull the girls away. I screamed for help, but the screech of the train's brakes muffled my cry. The throng of people all around us prevented me from seeing Murray up on the steps several yards in front of us. My attackers were on both sides, yanking at the girls as hard as they could. I intensified my grip on the girls' hands, terrified I would be separated from them. I was doing everything I could to hold on to my daughters. I was even kicking my attackers. They were skilled thieves and knew exactly what they were doing. The harder they yanked on the girls, the wider apart my arms stretched. My unguarded purse swung in front of me like a sacrificial lamb. In a split second, I realized they weren't really interested in the girls. The attackers wanted my purse. They knew I would not let go of the girls, and they were correct. Pulling the girls away from me was purely a diversionary tactic.

Helplessly, I watched as they skillfully whipped open my purse and pulled out my wallet. I started screaming at fever pitch, "HELP, I am being robbed!" It had all happened so quickly and the cacophony of the train station was so uproarious that Murray had not heard me let alone noticed what was going on. As quickly as they had encircled me, my assailants were gone. They had vanished into thin air with my wallet. I could hardly believe I had fallen victim to their ploy. Even more amazing, no one around us seemed to notice or care. They were totally focused on making it onto the train prior to its imminent departure. These thieves were pros, and they were long gone.

I smothered the girls with cuddles, so thankful they were still with me. Astonishingly, they both seemed okay, and so with no further ado, we again started jogging down the tracks toward Murray. It was time to focus all our energy on the task at hand: getting on the train before it left without us. We reached Murray in the nick of time. I handed the girls up, and he yanked me up behind them just as the train chugged out of the station.

"What took you so long?" he asked me as I began whimpering into his chest while I gathered the girls as close into us as possible.

I sniveled my way through an explanation of my twenty-second ordeal. I was relieved that we were finally on the train beside him. He held me tight, and I gathered myself together. I glanced down into my still-open purse with a smile. I had left the house with only my favorite strawberry lip gloss, a bottle of perfume, a comb, a handkerchief, and an almost empty wallet. The robbers had scored a few Romanian Lei, the equivalent of about two dollars. Long ago, we had worked out that whenever we were out in crowds together, big, tall Murray, who towered above most Romanians, would always tuck our money and credit cards deep inside his chest pocket where no one would dare to reach. Implementing this precaution meant that we had actually outfoxed the clever thieves. This sudden realization made me feel pretty chuffed. I did a tiny fist pump and broke into a little victory jig as the train rolled out of the station. Murray looked at me aghast.

"Are you sure you are alright?"

I nodded. Thankfully, the thieves had left my favorite lip gloss and perfume behind. I pulled them out of my purse, swiped the lip gloss across my still quivering lips, and thoroughly doused myself with perfume. All was okay. I was now ready for the next five hours of stinky train, followed by a lively weekend exploring a new city with friends. It was good to be married to a giant, but next time I would make sure we stuck closer to him all the way.

• • •

The genuinely special and amazing people we met along the way were one of the greatest benefits of living and working in Romania. Our friend Kirsten from Denmark fell into this category. She was a gentle, kind, brave, and quietly strong woman. Kirsten arrived in Romania by herself, hoping to adopt orphans. But this was no easy task. Every step along the way was fraught with difficulties and piles of red tape. Frequently, she was told she was crazy and that it was an impossible task to undertake as a single woman. But despite many setbacks and struggles, she eventually did exactly what she believed she should do. She set up an orphanage, legally adopted orphans, and offered them a loving and kind home in Romania, helping to heal and restore some of the damage that had been done to them from their cruel past. We greatly admired Kirsten. We supported her however we could. When we took mini-vacations, trips, or weekend getaways, we often invited Kirsten and her children to accompany us.

On one of these trips, we stumbled across a thermal spa at Hajdúszoboszló, a small town near Debrecen. Now I just love to soak in a hot tub and enjoy a full body massage. There is nothing more wonderful in the world. So the moment we heard about this nearby spa, I was like a horse heading for home. I bundled everyone into Candy within a flash and encouraged Murray to put pedal to the metal to get us there in record speed.

We had no idea what to expect. After we paid our entry fee, I waved goodbye to Murray. We were hustled through the doors to the women's area, and the boys were deftly steered to the men's area. Our guide was babbling to us in Hungarian while handing us what appeared to be signup papers with time slots. We deduced they wanted us to fill out a schedule for the various services on offer. We had not the foggiest idea what we might be subscribing to. What the heck! I decided to throw all caution to the wind and enroll in everything on the schedule. What could be bad about a day at the spa? Kirsten raised an eyebrow and declined the treatments, muttering to me she would be happy to hang out in the big pool with Murray and all the kids. It was her loss.

We headed further into the women's locker room. The kids started giggling. We were surrounded by big naked mamas hanging out and enjoying the comfort of the women's area as if they were sitting at the park, fully clothed on a sunny afternoon. Most of them had various shades of purplish-red, perfectly coiffed hair. This seemed to be the dominant Eastern European hair fashion for many middle-aged women at the time. Now I am not uncomfortable with nakedness, but the combination of massive jiggling breasts paired with purple coiffed hair staring at us from every angle was hilarious. The girls were right—this scene was giggle worthy. It was downright comical.

Before I realized where my mind was going, I shuddered ever so slightly at the vision that most probably confronted Murray in the men's area. Beefy, pot-bellied, naked men hanging around in all their glory! *Yikes! Focus, Leanne.*

The girls and I pulled on our very cute swimsuits and headed out to the unisex general pool area to meet up with Murray. I deposited them with their daddy, turned tail, and headed back into the women's area for my treatments. I was awash with excitement just thinking about the relaxing massage I was about to receive. I handed over my schedule and was ushered into a room that looked rather frighteningly like a concrete vault. A matronly looking woman told me to strip. Her tone indicated that I daren't hesitate for even a nanosecond. I peeled off my swimsuit in a jiffy. A moment later, another woman in a white plastic coat and white galoshes walked into the vault with what looked like a massive fire hose. She flicked a valve, aimed the nozzle straight at me, and pelted me with an unbelievably powerful turbo jet of ice-cold water. I gasped and then screamed some marvelous obscenity. What the hell was she doing?

"Tsk, tsk ,tsk," hissed the rather hefty woman who was manning the fire hose and aiming it at my slender white thighs. I tried to dodge the powerful ice jet, but to no avail. As I looked at her mean, gnarly face, I felt quite sure that this was personal and that she was trying to take me out. It was like we were playing a nasty game of hopscotch. The second I jumped to a new square, she aimed right at me and with exceptional precision, she shot me front, right, and center. I clearly could not win this game. So I summoned up all my powers of endurance, breathed deeply, and let the white-coated female Darth Vader enjoy herself. I had to acquiesce in order to survive. It was time to give in and fake enjoyment. A huge smile spread over her face.

When she ceased with the fire hose torture, I was handed a rather scratchy, whitish looking towel. I tried to suppress my shivering because I wasn't exactly sure whether it was a result of the icy-cold-water blasts or because of the sheer terror of what might lie ahead for me in the next chamber of horrors. Cautiously, I tiptoed into the next room. I was told to lie flat on my stomach on a stone bench. I knew not to question the command. One second later, I was stark naked and prostrate. I nervously glanced to the right of me and noticed some grave-looking implements laid out on a table beside the bench. Enter the sorcerer's apprentice! Holy crap! She elegantly fingered a few instruments and then after a terrifyingly long pause, she slowly picked up what appeared to be a gigantic pumice stone. For the next twenty minutes, she proceeded, with great gusto, to scrub me from head to toe. Boy did I tingle. I almost convinced myself that it felt pretty good. I wondered if this was perhaps because I was still numb from the ice-water blasts. Who cared at this point? So I settled in and embraced the deepest exfoliation possible, short of being skinned alive.

Then I passed through a deliciously warm steam room. Now we were talking. This was my kind of spa. Eventually, I was dragged from my bliss and guided toward my final stop: the massage table. A herculean woman gave me what was possibly the most powerful massage in history. It was amazing. When she was through, I tentatively wobbled back up onto my feet, pulled on my cute little swimsuit, and glided back to the general pool area to join my family.

Murray asked me how the treatments went, and I managed a few monosyllabic grunts with my tongue slightly lolling out of my mouth. It was rare for me not to have something to say. He looked at me with mild alarm. I managed to squeak out the words "torture chamber." He let out a somewhat muffled whistle, and a big smile spread across his handsome face.

"Glad you had fun," he said as I fell feebly onto a lounge chair and slept for the rest of the afternoon.

· · ·

Mamaia is a beach resort town near Constanța on the shore of the Black Sea. During Communist rule, it was a vacation spot for the ruling Romanian Communist Party elite. It was considered Romania's most beautiful seaside resort. Since I just loved anything to do with the ocean and the beach, we decided we needed to take a trip. It was a nine-hour drive from Cluj to Mamaia, but that did not deter us. We invited Kirsten and her family to come along. Once again, we all piled into Candy and set out on a harrowing drive to our summer vacation destination.

We learned from our Romanian friends that securing a hotel room in Mamaia was no easy feat. In fact, it had to be done months ahead of time. All bookings were made through the state-owned travel agency. There was no guarantee you would stay at a specific hotel. We made our booking, paid our money—at the highly inflated rate that all foreigners had to pay—and secured our lodgings.

We entered the lobby of our rather tired-looking hotel and handed over the papers showing our prepaid reservations. We were merrily informed by the perky desk clerk that we did not have a reservation, even if the paperwork said so. We needed to pay more money if we wished to lodge at this hotel for the next few days.

Was she kidding?

We were hot and tired. This information did not sit well with me. After hours of travel, the kids were wired and at the point where tears could erupt at the slightest provocation. Murray serenely told the desk clerk that we did have a reservation and once again pointed to the documentation. She bristled a little and told us to step aside and wait while she sorted things out.

So we did. It took quite some time to realize she was not in fact trying to sort it out at all. She was just booking lots of other happy vacationers into their rooms and had completely forgotten all about our rambunctious little party. I was really annoyed. Booking papers in hand, I marched back up to the desk clerk ready to do battle.

"Hello," she said in her sweetest voice without even looking up at me. "Welcome to our hotel, and how can I help you?" Was she kidding? She was pretending we had not already been through this scenario exactly fifteen minutes ago. I summoned all the sweetness I could muster and took a deep breath. Once again, I explained we were keen to get to our rooms and did not wish to stand aside any longer. We had waited long enough. She raised her gaze, locked eyes with me, and glared.

Silently, I glared back. After what seemed like an eternity, she finally blinked, dropped her gaze a smidge, and said that perhaps she could get a hold of the supervisor.

"Yes that would be great," I replied as I fake smiled at her. I could feel the ice water surging through my veins.

She marched off and returned with her supervisor, who explained to me that the hotel was indeed full. I told her that was not my problem because we had a reservation. We were not leaving, so she had better find a way to sort it out for us. After much harrumphing, flipping of pages in the large reservations book on the desk, and some surreptitious whispering between themselves, she told me they might be able to work something out.

"That would be splendid," I replied, honeyed kindness dripping from my tongue. My glare remained rock hard. In the background, I heard an almost inaudible whistle escape from Murray's lips. He knew the desk clerk had met her match with me.

Of course I knew exactly what they wanted to "work out." They wanted a big fat bribe! To be honest, we had already overpaid to stay there and we just did not have spare resources to pay more money to fatten some annoying hotel employee's pockets. The only thing I could do was tell them that even though we looked like rich tourists, we in fact were not.

"We live in Romania and have very limited resources and have already overpaid and are not paying a single penny more." My voice rose to what sounded like fever pitch. When I turned around to see if I could herald up some support, the people in line behind me looked down at the floor to avoid eye contact. Oh no, I was being the crazy woman again.

I had made quite a scene and could tell they wanted to be rid of us. Clearly, I was not going to budge one inch from my place at the check-in desk until they resolved this matter. With another round of harrumphing and page turning, the supervisor eventually "found" us rooms and checked us in. We were told that our rooms would be ready in just ten minutes. They asked us to quietly step aside to the waiting area. I firmly held my ground at the front desk until the woman behind the counter informed us just how lucky we were that our rooms were now ready. The twitching clerk shooed us away.

As one can imagine, the rooms were nothing like the ones we had actually booked. We had paid for oceanview suites. Our "sea view" captured the laundry and kitchen area of the hotel perfectly. Murray giggled. "Love the view," he chortled. The rooms were tiny. Extra beds had been shoved into every spare inch. I think we may have just been sent to the staff quarters. The kids were already somersaulting across the wall of beds, not in the slightest bit perturbed by our new digs. "Time to make the most of a funny situation," suggested Murray. He was right, and a teeny-weeny smile crept onto my lips at Mr. Calm's perspective.

By now the fight had gone out of me. This was as good as we would get. We were so tired that I just didn't care about our insalubrious accommodations anymore. At least we were at the seaside, we had rooms, and we weren't relegated to spending the night in Candy. Perhaps they had a rather clever strategy after all. Use the fear of having nowhere to stay and make us wait long enough, and we would be happy with anything.

It was actually quite hilarious when Kirsten pulled back the sheets that night to get into her bed and found a pair of men's boxer shorts under the covers. We knew the hotel was punishing us for failing to stump up a bribe. We called housekeeping and the front desk several times to remedy the issue, but of course no one ever picked up. Finally too tired to care anymore, the boxer shorts were thrown aside and we all snuggled into the lumpy beds and fell fast asleep. Living in Romania was just one strange adventure after another.

• • •

Our modern society frequently teaches us that using our thinking powers alone is what really matters. Smart, thinking, normal people don't rely on intuition. We are taught there is a "normal and right way" to do things, a "normal" way to act and to live. Many are afraid of stepping outside of that norm. Many people fear taking risks or listening to their intuition. They shut it down the moment it starts to speak.

As a result, they never move into that wonderful realm of freedom and growth that results from acting on intuition.

Listening to your *inner voice* and following an unknown path can be intensely difficult. Sometimes it opens up areas in your life you would rather ignore. But I can attest that in the long run it is 100 percent worth following. The next period of our lives was one of those extremely difficult times. It took some time, but eventually we made it through difficult and into wonderful.

At some point early in 1998, Murray and I began to feel it was time to leave Romania. We had given a lot of ourselves over the past few years. We were tired, and we felt we needed to get our girls back into a traditional schooling environment. We started looking for the next step in our journey.

We owned a flat in Scotland, but it was rented out. Our renters wanted to stay on. We were not feeling a draw to return there. We did not feel it was time to return to Canada or New Zealand. We really weren't sure what was ahead, but we were aware of that voice telling us that change was afoot.

We had met a British couple from Worthing, England, the previous year. They ran a nonprofit in Eastern Europe, and on their travels they had stayed with us several times. They knew we were considering leaving Romania and invited us to work with them at their headquarters in Worthing.

After much consideration, we decided to move to Worthing. Murray would get a job working as a software engineer, and I would work with the nonprofit. We gave away almost everything that we had amassed while living in Transylvania, and for the final time Murray performed his packing magic on Candy.

Leaving Romania was very emotional for me. I had fallen deeply in love with this country. Its people would be in my heart forever. Living there had touched me in a way that had permanently impacted my life. We left with very little external wealth, but we were internally rich beyond belief. It was a season of my life I would not have changed for all the riches in the world.

CHAPTER 16

· · · · · · · · · · · · · · · · ·

A Fireball of Anger and a Glimmer of Hope

Five days later, we rolled into Worthing, an English seaside town. Little did we know just how difficult the next several months would be.

We rented and moved into a small two-bedroom apartment. The first night we discovered that the whole apartment was infested with fleas. While we had lived in far worse conditions in Romania with no power or running water, having fleas jump all over the girls in my home left me feeling disgusted. Thank God for exterminators and flea bombs.

The school that came highly recommended to us had an opening for Julia but not for Victoria. We had no choice but to enroll the girls in different schools. Julia's new school was awesome; Victoria's was not. Julia thrived in her new life; Victoria did not. My mothering mind started to fill with guilt. What had we done? Niggles of doubt about our move to Worthing infiltrated my thinking.

To get a good job, Murray quickly realized that he needed to update his skills. Software engineering is a fast-moving field, and his skills were a bit rusty after several years of working outside of that discipline. Despite his concerted efforts, he had not found a job. It was worrying.

I began my new job with the nonprofit organization and quickly found it was not a good fit in more ways than one. Eventually, after failing to make the job a success, I terminated my employment. It was a most unsettling development. We had primarily relocated to Worthing for this job. I wondered, *Did we get it wrong? Perhaps we should not have come to Worthing.*

Then I received some disturbing news from the property manager of our Paisley flat. Recently, there had been a water leak in the kitchen. The plumber had opened the wall to fix the leak and had discovered dry rot. A more in-depth investigation uncovered that a fast-moving fungus had riddled the framework of our entire flat. They'd have to replace the framework and the entire bathroom and kitchen. These were major renovations; the huge quotes we received from contractors reflected this.

When we realized our tenants would have to vacate the flat for several months to make room for the repairs, my mood plummeted to a new low. Our financial situation scared me. Neither Murray nor I had jobs. We owned a now-vacant flat with a mortgage payment, and we had to make costly repairs. Additionally, we had living expenses in Worthing. We had no idea how we were going to afford it all.

Then a few weeks later one frigid February day, Mum called and told me that one of my closest friends in New Zealand had just been diagnosed with terminal cancer. He had less than six weeks to live. I hung up the phone, sat on the floor, and wept like I hadn't wept in a very long time. I wept for the loss of my dear friend. I wept for his wife and their three little boys who would be left without their beloved husband and father. I wept for my Victoria who was so lonely and unhappy with her school and our living situation. I wept over our lack of success in securing good jobs. I wept over the hefty debt we were all too quickly amassing. It was as though the floodgates had opened. I felt great sorrow and out it flowed in great rivers of tears. I felt very alone, as though I had descended into a very dark place.

• • •

It was such a relief when a software engineering company in Brighton eventually hired Murray. His new position included a retraining program to update his skills and bring him back up to speed with new programming languages. It was perfect but with one caveat: Upon completion of his retraining, he had to fulfill a one-year contract with his new company where they could send him to work anywhere in the UK. The idea of moving again filled me with dread. Recently, I had found myself languishing in an emotionally low place. My internal resources were depleted, and the mere thought of finding the energy to move again filled me with fear. As best I could, I pushed these thoughts out of my mind and tried to be thankful for Murray's new job. I would face the next chapter when it arose.

Murray worked very long hours. He labored to get through the retraining program as rapidly as possible, because only then would his salary substantially increase. We had a huge repair bill to pay, and we desperately needed the income. He came home from the office late one evening and suggested we sit down for a chat once the girls were in bed. I knew he had completed his training and was awaiting placement on his first project. His tone captured my attention.

"The company wants me to move to America for a project," he said with a big swallow. Blood rushed to my ears and sirens wailed in my head.

"What did you just say?" I croaked. "The United States . . . of America?" Surely I had misunderstood him.

Gently, he explained that his company had recently opened their first US office in Raleigh, North Carolina. They had sent several employees from the Brighton office headquarters to work there. Unfortunately, a few of the employees had some visa restriction issues, which meant they had to return to the UK. Quite simply, the new US office was now understaffed. The CEO had approached Murray that day and asked him to fill one of the vacant positions in the USA. With a Canadian passport, it would be more straightforward to obtain a work visa. He had the necessary skills to fill the position. He had aced the training, had more life experience than many of the other employees, and had previously lived in cross-cultural settings. The CEO thought the job was perfect for him. The only hitch was that they needed him there immediately. Oh, and one more thing: The position was initially only for six months. There was a possibility that it could be extended, but no guarantees.

My mouth dropped open. I just stared at him. Was he freaking serious? He was actually thinking about leaving us for six months. He read my expression and gently put his arm around my quivering shoulders. Big tears once again rolled down my cheeks.

"No," he explained. "You and the girls would come too. I wouldn't leave you behind. The company will relocate us all to the States, but I have to give them an answer in two days. I would leave in just over a week."

Suddenly I was so angry. All the fear I had felt from the past few months welled up inside of me and turned into a great big fireball of rage. I couldn't believe Murray had come to me with this stupid notion. How could he want to uproot everything again? In reality, we did not have any "roots" in Worthing at all. But I could not see that in the heat of the moment. I wasn't thinking straight. I was afraid and irrational. I yelled at him. I made it clear I categorically was NOT moving to the USA. How could he even think I would consider it? I did not want to talk to him about it again. End of the matter. I ran out the door, jumped into Candy, slammed her into reverse, and skidded out the driveway. I headed to the beach for a long walk on the cold, windy, rocky English seashore under the stars.

I stayed out late that night as I grappled with something unraveling deep inside of me. I cried hot, angry tears. The past several months had been difficult. I was extremely unhappy with where we had landed and the lack of opportunities. I had come here expecting good things. Instead, it had been a horrible several months. I did not have a job, and Victoria was still deeply unhappy. I felt resentful. We had given so much of ourselves over the years, doing what we felt sure we should be doing for others. Shouldn't things be easier for us now? We had followed what we thought was our *inner voice* and moved to Worthing. So far it had turned out to be a disastrous decision. I couldn't understand why. I felt so forgotten by the universe. My normally positive outlook on life had vanished. I was angry and afraid. I hated living in Worthing. But moving to the USA? Was Murray insane?

I arrived home in the wee hours of the night and tucked myself into bed. In his own quiet and wise way, "Murray the Calm" did not say anything more to me. He just gently stroked my head as my tears silently oozed onto my pillow. He knew that for some reason this suggestion had really, really, really upset me. I'm sure my reaction completely confounded him. It wasn't normal, and I knew that. But there it was. I was having a deeply visceral reaction to what he considered a seemingly great opportunity. He knew to give me space, and I would work through things.

The following morning, he silently hugged me for a long time before rolling out of bed. He tootled off to Brighton on the train without mentioning a thing about moving. He could see I was wrestling with demons and that I needed time to deal with them. Once I had dropped the girls off at school and was alone, I asked myself questions. *Why am I flipping out over this? Why would it be so terrible to move to the USA? After all, we had moved to the UK and then Romania when the girls were babies and we had no resources. This is America. Won't that be a whole lot easier?* Slowly, as the day rolled on, I realized I was kicking against this idea because it was more change, more uncertainty. I didn't want more change. I was afraid, I was tired, and I had allowed fear to take a deep hold of me. Living in the USA was totally foreign to me. I had never even heard of freaking Raleigh! I was afraid that it might not work out well, just as our move to Worthing had not. I was worried for the girls. It distressed me to think about uprooting them again. This move would be temporary. I wanted permanent. I wanted settled, happy, and easy. It all came down to fear. I was afraid of the unknown and the possibility of things turning out worse than I felt they already were.

I had allowed adversity to fuel lies to which I had listened. I had second-guessed my ability to truly hear my *inner voice*. I doubted our decision to move to Worthing, even though we had felt so sure we should make the move. I let my difficult circumstances wreak havoc with my faith. I allowed myself to spiral into a dark place. But now it was time to let go of my anger and fear.

After we put our girls to bed, Murray sat down with me. He gently held my hands and said, "I know you don't feel happy about things here, and I know you don't want to think about another move, but I am quite sure this is the right opportunity for us. We should all go to the USA."

At the very moment he spoke those simple words, I knew deep down inside of me that he was right. He did not attempt to coerce me. He knows I need to believe in something myself before I will commit to it. In all our years together, we had always come to decisions together. This time was different. Murray was sure we should go to the USA. Even though I was not there yet, the strength of conviction in his voice garnered my complete and utter attention. Something in my heart whispered that I should listen to him. For the first time in many, many months, I heard my *inner voice* and I knew deep inside that this was the path we should follow. Murray was 100 percent right. Even though it was all a vast unknown right now, I trusted that it would be the best possible thing for all of us. It was time to stop being scared. It was time to trust in the *power of things unseen.*

We had just made the momentous decision to move our family to the USA with no idea what really lay ahead. All we could see was that Murray had a job in Raleigh for the next six months. There was nothing more. Once again, we were taking a great big leap into the unknown with almost no resources to speak of. We had nothing more to go on than a deep inner sense that this was the right thing for us to do.

Not surprisingly, I felt a tremendous relief about leaving Worthing after we decided to move. A glimmer of excitement over this decision slowly grew inside of me until it was a bright, shining blaze. England was no longer the place for us. An amazing realization struck me: If we had not moved to Worthing, the opportunity to move to the US and start the next amazing leg of our lives would never have happened. We had seen this phenomenon before, and here it was happening again. It had indeed been the right move for us, despite the struggles we had endured.

Sometimes, we have very dim times in our lives. It is just how life goes. This was one of those times. But I had hung on. I had wobbled a lot, but in the end I had not lost faith. I had cried a lot, but I had not given up when it felt dark to me. I had hung on believing for a miracle, and then all of a sudden one appeared. Moving to the United States of America was completely different from anything I could have ever dreamed up. It had been nowhere on my radar, and yet it was the perfect miracle for our entire family.

A new journey to a new country was beginning.

CHAPTER 17

. . . .

A Mountain of Food and a Needle in a Haystack

It was so wonderful to finally arrive at Raleigh-Durham International Airport. Murray had already been in the USA for six weeks. The girls and I had stayed behind in the UK so they could finish the school term and I could tie up all our affairs there.

In the past six weeks, Murray had not only worked long hours at his new job, but he had made time for house hunting as well. Initially, he had looked at rentals, but then he discovered something quite surprising: His job allowed him to qualify for a loan to purchase a home with almost no down payment. It would be more affordable for us than renting. He had a one-year work visa, had only been in the USA a few weeks, and had no credit history, but somehow he still got approved to buy a home. Amazing!

On one of our many phone calls when the girls and I were still overseas, Murray and I had talked about the unknowns of our situation. He only had a one-year visa, and my visa would not allow me to work. Because Murray's job was initially only for six months, should we be making a thirty-year mortgage commitment? It seemed a bit crazy to purchase a home with such tentative plans. But there it was again, that voice inside of us. We couldn't shake it. We felt we should make a bold move and purchase a home rather than rent.

The girls and I ran through the airport doors to Murray, excited to see him again after the weeks apart. He enfolded the three of us with a massive Canadian bear hug and smothered us with sweet kisses. He had a huge smile. I felt all gooey inside just to be beside my gentle giant again.

In just three days, we were due to close on our new home. In the meantime, we would crash at a hotel for a couple of days and start to get acquainted with our new hometown.

We had arrived in Raleigh in the evening, and the girls and I were ready to fall into bed for a good night's sleep. But we were starving after our travels, so we set out to get something to eat before turning in for the night. As luck would have it, a restaurant stood right across the street from our hotel. It had massive, gaudy signs emblazoned across every window advertising an "All-You-Can-Eat Buffet $6.99." In my slightly disoriented, travel-wearied state, a quick meal sounded like a good idea. I imagined we would not have to wait for our food and that we could make it back to our hotel beds with a full stomach in next to no time.

So we made a beeline straight for the welcoming doors across the road. My tummy rumbled loudly. I could not wait to eat my first meal in America. My mouth watered. We eagerly threw open the doors and entered the restaurant. The tableau that greeted my eyes was quite simply astounding. Perhaps I was just plain exhausted and suffering from jet lag so my perception of things was a little off-kilter. But no, the scene really was startling. In terms of restaurants, it was like nothing I had ever seen before. It were as if we had just landed in a restaurant superstore. Long bars overflowed with steaming hot vittles, massive islands full of seafood, unending stations of meats, salads, and vegetables, and huge baskets of bread, rolls, and muffins. Tables were groaning under the sheer weight of the desserts, ice cream, and candies resting atop them. Everywhere the eye could behold, there was food. Mountains of it.

Perhaps this was all the more amazing to me because of our relatively recent experience in Romania, where it had been difficult to find food. We had never been to an all-you-can-eat buffet restaurant of this magnitude. So when I stepped into this scene, feeling slightly wobbly on my feet, I was gobsmacked.

We made it to a table and sat. I continued to stare at the picture in front of me. In addition to the heaving quantities of food, I now noticed something else: Alarmingly large people ambitiously piled their already laden plates to overflowing. They then headed back to their tables, where they scoffed down their food in record time so they could jump back up and nearly run back for the next load. Ridiculous!

This scene quashed all thoughts of my hunger. I could not stop staring. My jaw dropped, and I let out a low long "whoa . . ." Murray nudged me, discreetly shook his head, and with his lovely green eyes, told me not to be so damn rude. Despite his inconspicuous rebuke, I noticed his large grin and the twinkle of amusement in his eyes. The thought went through my head, *Why do people need* so much *food?*

Once I became accustomed to my surroundings, I finally stopped gawking. What the heck, it was time to eat like an American! I grabbed a plate and joined the other diners in my quest for food. As I worked my way through the line, I was struck with an interesting realization. In the past twelve months, we had lived in a country racked by extreme poverty and need. Now we were living in the richest country on the planet. If I had tried to create a detailed plan of my life, I could never have come up with the story that was unfolding in front of me. I had been on a mighty adventure, all because I had followed my instincts and listened to that still small voice inside. Sometimes the route was circuitous, as the past few months had proved. I had definitely been through ups and downs. That is how life goes. New things were about to unfold. It was good to be alive, living my life, living my story, even though it was one that was far from normal.

• • •

When we arrived at the new home Murray had picked out, we gave him a big thumbs-up for a job well done. After the many places we had resided, this one was by far the best. It was a brand-new four-bedroom home nestled on four wooded acres just outside the city. The girls had their own bedrooms for the first time, much to their delight. After months of feeling so very unsettled, I couldn't wait to make my own nest.

On one of our long phone calls over the previous weeks, Murray had asked me what my dream home would look like. Well, he had found it in aces. It was beyond my wildest dreams. After all we had been through over the past few months, it was truly an oasis.

We had promised the girls a puppy as soon as we got settled. Murray found one before we arrived in the USA and had her waiting for our arrival at the new house. You can only imagine our girls' sheer delight upon meeting the newest family member. That first night, we had nothing more than the contents of our suitcases and one very cute puppy. We did not have a stick of furniture. We really were starting from scratch. When it was time for bed, Julia snuggled her fur baby into an empty, open suitcase. She then tucked her sweaters around the puppy and declared that our new family member had the best doggie bed in town. She was correct. However, the human members of the family did not have beds. So the four of us pulled on our PJs, lay down on the carpet, and covered ourselves with big winter coats for bedclothes. Naturally, the girls thought this "indoor camping" sleeping arrangement was absolutely terrific.

I lay on the carpet in front of the fireplace, mesmerized by its dancing flames. I was curled up in Murray's arms, so thankful to be together again. I whispered, "I feel like we are immigrants that just got off the boat." Then it struck me. We *are* immigrants! What an adventure we were on. It was magnificent.

• • •

It was December, and Christmas was fast approaching. Despite our limited possessions, I was determined to make it a special holiday. As was our custom, I planned to cook a large traditional turkey dinner. By Christmas Eve, the fridge was stocked to bursting. I swear it was so stuffed you could almost hear it groaning. The girls and I baked up a storm, and the pantry was full of delicious mouth-watering goodies. Murray cut down a small pine tree on our property, à la Charlie Brown. We convinced the girls that this spindly specimen would make a fine Christmas tree and trimmed it with a few beautiful baubles. Despite the fact it was so skinny, the tree looked festive in a funny sort of way. By Christmas Eve, gifts magically appeared under the glittering tree. Our house was filled with excitement. The girls' expectations of a joyous morning ahead were palpable.

But then something quite unexpected happened. On Christmas Eve, it rained unceasingly for hours. As the night wore on, the temperatures began to plummet. The heavy precipitation turned to freezing rain, which left a thick layer of ice over everything.

In the dawn hours of Christmas morning, we awoke to terrifically loud cracking sounds. We arose from our warm beds to a frigid house, not sure what was happening. When we looked out the windows, we found a winter wonderland. The world was coated in inches of ice creating a spectacular panorama. As the rain slowly ceased, the sun peeked through the heavy clouds and sparkled through the ice crystals in a truly magnificent display. It was as though light was shining through a prism, creating a million dazzling colors. But despite the unbridled beauty that had revealed itself to us that morning, havoc was advancing. Thirty-foot pine trees were bent over and almost touching the ground. The weight of the ice grew too heavy for the trees and power lines, eventually snapping them in half as if they were toothpicks. This was the unfamiliar cracking sound to which we had awoken. Showers of splintering ice exploded into the air as huge limbs toppled to the ground.

We lost power to our home for our first American Christmas. The turkey remained untrussed in the fridge, and the temperature indoors began to plunge. As an eternally optimistic person, I kept reassuring everyone that the power would be back on in no time and our Christmas activities could advance with full vigor. Undeterred by the cold, our girls unwrapped their gifts with little fingers that shivered from both excitement and the arcticlike clime. It was so cold inside that we finally donned our warm outdoor gear and went for a long walk in the glistening, enchanted world outside. If nothing else, brisk exercise would increase the blood flow in our shivery bodies and halt our teeth from chattering. It was a staggeringly beautiful walk.

However, on our return, my optimistic predictions did not materialize. We still had no electricity. Our little gas fireplace was having no impact on the tumbling temperatures inside our open-plan home. It was freezing, and our body temps had cooled down to polar levels. Despite layers of clothes that made us look like the Michelin Man family, we just couldn't get warm. Sadly, the turkey was not going to make it out of the fridge and into the oven in time for Christmas dinner. It was time to abandon the house and take up residence in our car. We turned up the heat to full blast and headed out in search of a restaurant that would provide us with a much needed warm Christmas dinner.

It's amazing how challenging it is to find a restaurant that is open on Christmas day. Throw into the mix that we were in an unfamiliar city—"Just Google it" wasn't quite yet a reality—and our search became nigh impossible. In addition, many of the areas in which we scouted for eateries had also lost power. Everything in the city had ground to a complete stop.

We drove—more like slid, truth be told—through icy and deserted city streets, scouring the shop fronts for any sign of life or food. Suddenly, all three of us starving girls screamed out in unison for Murray to stop the car. We had just found the proverbial needle in a haystack: an open Chinese restaurant. Murray slid to a halt. We all dove out of the car to check out our find. Our elation knew no limits when we realized that we had hit the jackpot. The restaurant was indeed open and warm. We could see huge steaming dishes of Chinese cuisine being ferried to overcrowded tables. Within minutes, we were ushered to the only empty table left in the restaurant. It was fantastic to be served bowl after bowl of hot Chinese deliciousness. We savored the most gratifying Christmas dinner we had ever eaten. We made that meal last a very long time. It felt so good to be warm, and we were so merry to enjoy the most unusual yuletide dinner we had had to date.

When we finally got home, the house was still dark and exceptionally cold; but our bellies were full, and we had enjoyed a jubilant family day together. We were so lucky to have each other. Within an hour, the power suddenly flickered back on. It was late, and it was time for bed. Happy, sated, and weary, we all hit the sack with big smiles. Our totally unplanned, impromptu Christmas was the best ever. Funny how that works. As I thought about it, I realized it was a little comment on life.

Sometimes the best outcomes occur when your plans go awry. Going with the flow often brings us the most joy.

I love that life is full of unpredictable surprises, big and small. They are there for us to relish as they come our way.

· · ·

We quickly settled into our new life in North Carolina. It was a very happy time. The girls started the New Year at a great school where they were warmly welcomed. Phew! What a relief.

Our neighbors were amazing. They turned up at our door to offer us help with settling in. We have always had all that we've needed for a particular moment in time. It was happening again. New place, new needs, but the same perfect provisions all along the way.

I often think this has something to do with our expectations. If we believe something will happen, we open up the possibility of it coming to fruition. When I have needs, I have learned to be open in my thinking and to expect new things. I have also learned not to put limits on the answers and not to arrive at a situation with preconceptions. Just enjoy life with an open heart and mind, and watch miracles unfold.

This is one of the great things about stepping into an unknown situation: We open the door for unexpected blessings to come our way. Complete strangers have often given to us in our time of need. It is wonderful.

So often today, we are taught we should have it all together; we should not need help. This is a flawed mentality. It is not healthy to be isolated from our fellow man and to go through life needing no one. Whether we believe it or not, we are all family. We need one another. It is truly wonderful to have our lives interconnected with others, to give and receive. This is how it is meant to be.

I love knowing I am part of this universe and that the very essence of who I am is interconnected with others. If we follow the unique path that is within each of us, we will find many others along the way with whom we can connect. We will have deep and meaningful relationships. No amount of success, riches, fame, or glamour can replace this. I am deeply thankful for all the people I have met—people who follow their path as I follow mine. We enrich one another. Our journeys are interconnected. Beautiful!

CHAPTER 18

· · · · · · · · · · · · · · · · ·

Goosebumps and Living the Good Life

Murray's six-month job turned into several years. I was residing in America on a dependent visa, which did not allow me to work. Initially, that was okay. I enjoyed being a stay-at-home mom. It was wonderful to have so much time with the girls and to enjoy a simpler life for a season.

But before long, I was ready for more of a challenge. I had no idea what that might be. Unless I could obtain a different visa or a green card, I could not legally work. The process of securing a green card was long and tedious and required a job offer in a shortage profession. Physiotherapy was considered a shortage profession, but my New

Zealand qualification was not recognized in the States. To work in my field, I would have to go back to school for a few years. That idea didn't gel with me. It felt like a backward step to retrain in a profession that I had worked in for fifteen years and across three countries. So I ruled it out. I was sure there was something else out there. I would wait and keep looking for employment possibilities. In the meantime, I would continue to enjoy all that I had around me.

The following summer, the CEO of Murray's company flew in from the UK to visit the Raleigh office. I was invited to attend a dinner for the employees. Somehow I ended up sitting beside the CEO, who was a very interesting character. We got to chatting, and I told him a little about myself and my family's adventures over the years. Half an hour later, as I was regaling him with some crazy story about one of our shenanigans, he leaned toward me and said, "Leanne, would you be interested in working in marketing and recruitment for my company?"

"Excuse me?" I squeaked with shock. I had adopted that convenient American phrase, and it popped out of my mouth in a ridiculous-sounding high pitch.

"You know, work here for my company. We are ready to expand, and we have decided to create a full-time position in marketing and recruitment for our US office," he said, his very British accent sounding like his words were about to be swallowed.

Whaaaat? Was he serious? *Breathe. Stop gaping. Answer him!*

"I would love to," I said, settling my vocal chords in a manner that would make Mr. Calm proud, "except I have no training in that area and have no work visa for the USA. But thanks so much for such a terrific offer."

"I think you would be perfect for the position," he continued undeterred. "From what you have told me, it sounds as though a lot of what you were doing in the nonprofit arena in Europe was networking, marketing, and recruiting. I think you have the people skills to do the job. Forget formal training! I will send you back to the UK for a bit of training, and we will have you up to speed in no time."

Wow, that was a vote of confidence from someone who had known me for all of thirty minutes. My mind was spinning with what had just unfolded in the past two minutes.

"If you'd like the job, it's yours. I'll talk with my immigration attorney tomorrow and have her apply for an executive visa for you. We need someone with your international experience and skill to take this on."

And within a flash, I was hired for my new job as vice president of marketing and recruitment for an international software company! I jumped up and down inside, wanting to shriek with excitement. Instead, I kept demurely chatting with my new boss as though nothing out of the ordinary had just occurred. Indeed, if history is indicative, this was my "ordinary." Silly me for being taken by surprise when something wonderful happened. When would I learn to not be surprised by the *power of things unseen*? Who would have thought that this was the new direction my life would take? Definitely not me.

I loved that job. It suited my personality, and I enjoyed the challenge of doing something new. I was so grateful that Murray had sat me down that day in Worthing and expressed his strong conviction that he should take the job offer in America, despite the unfounded fury of my reaction. My gratitude knew no limits.

• • •

But as you know, life is always changing. A few years later, our company decided to relocate their US office from Raleigh to Washington, DC.

Murray and I drove up to DC for a few days to look at homes and schools. Despite the fact that our jobs would be there, we just couldn't get excited about moving to the area. Our girls were settled and happy in school. On this occasion, another move did not feel like the right thing to do. Teenage years are hard enough for any kid. We didn't feel it was the time to uproot Victoria and Julia again. We decided not to move with our jobs, which meant it was time to find new ones.

By this time we had green cards, so we were no longer restricted to working for the company that sponsored our initial visas. Murray quickly got a job as a software engineer with a new company. I had absolutely no idea what to do. I started looking for jobs, but even though I had vast experience in several areas, I did not have the US qualifications to get past the application process in most instances.

One day while riding horses at a friend's farm, the idea hit me: *What about real estate?* Where in the blazes did that come from? I had never considered selling real estate, but I just couldn't shake the thought. Before I knew it, I had enrolled in classes, passed the real estate licensing exam, and was hired as a real estate agent. I loved it. My new career started to blossom. A few weeks after embarking on this new path, I decided to get my broker's license and started a night class. Four months after the real estate career possibility had popped into my brain, I became a broker.

Within a couple of months, my new business was booming. Unfortunately, I was not all that happy with the company I had joined. One day, I had a really crazy thought: Maybe I should start my own company! I mulled this over for a week or two and chatted it through with Murray. He has a great business brain and loves working on details. He assured me that he would happily take care of all the paperwork involved in setting up a new real estate company for me. He thought it a brilliant idea and was confident I could make it a success. My rock. My ever-supportive, kind husband is always one to think big and to believe in me.

I was having lunch the following week with a colleague. Out of the blue, she mentioned that she was also feeling very unsettled with our company. She felt it was time to make some changes and was checking out some new possibilities. Interesting. I felt a little quiver and noticed my arms had gone all goosebumpy.

Tentatively, I told her I was pursuing the possibility of starting my own company. I was convinced she would consider me straight-out looney tunes. After all, I had next to no experience. But she did not appear to think I was insane. As we chatted, it dawned on me that we were on the same wavelength. I felt this unbelievable sense of unbridled excitement just well up inside me. Hard to explain, but there it was. I knew what it meant. We were going to work together. I was so excited that I could hardly eat my lunch. As anyone who knows me will tell you, it is a rare and shocking occasion when I can't eat delicious fare right smack in front of me. Something was definitely stirring.

Joni is one of the sweetest and kindest people I have ever met. She was a local and well-respected in our community. She had the connections I lacked. By the time we had finished lunch that auspicious day, we decided to partner up and start a new real estate company in our town. I floated out of the restaurant, all aglow with this sensational decision. I knew it was right. In fact, it was perfect.

We knew very little about running a real estate company or even about one another. We were nothing more than acquaintances. In some ways it was a bit like my marriage to Murray. We didn't know each other very well when we decided to get married, but I just knew it was the right thing to do. It called for a jump off the deep end. Here I was facing a similar choice. On both occasions it was not a leap of blind faith, because I knew inside me what I needed to do. Joni was an angel sent my way.

Just six months after I passed my real estate licensing exam, we opened the doors to our new real estate company. We rented a tiny space in an insurance office and started our business on a shoestring budget.

We were hungry for business and knocked on every door we could. We threw ourselves into our new company with great vigor.

There was a lot of new construction going on in our area, and I realized how much I enjoyed selling newly built homes. One word was screaming in my brain: OPPORTUNITY! I was particularly interested in one subdivision where construction had just begun. I had heard that the developer was looking for a new real estate company to market and sell the homes. So I called him several times and left messages. No reply. I sent him emails. No reply. I decided to track him down. I was like a dog with a bone. I drove over to the subdivision every single day to see if he was there. After doing this for a few weeks, I got lucky. One day, he was meeting with some of the city's building officials at the site. I waited until they were done and then I pounced, like a cat on a mouse. To be honest, I think I had worn him down with all my calls and messages. So when he finally met me, he listened patiently. I explained how much I loved new construction and wanted a chance to show him what I could do to sell his subdivision. Of course I left out the part that I had almost no experience. To my utter and complete astonishment, instead of telling me he was not interested, he said I could come to his office the following morning at nine a.m. He would give me a few minutes to present my marketing plan.

"Terrific," I chirped. Where had my voice gone? Why was I staring at him in total wonder? *Breathe, Leanne.* My mouth dropped open a tad, and I quickly snapped it shut. I summoned my calm powers and replied in a voice register that actually belonged to me, "That would be fantastic, thanks. You won't be disappointed. See you tomorrow at nine."

With my heart in full palpitation mode, I flew out of that subdivision at breakneck speed and skidded to a halt outside our tiny closet-sized office. All in a dither, I squealed, "Joni, we have an appointment with Larry tomorrow at nine to present our marketing plan."

"What plan?" she questioned.

"Exactly!" I screeched. "We need to come up with one, and it's already five p.m.!"

We set to work, building a marketing plan and presentation with almost no resources. When I got home later that evening, Murray, the software whiz, got on his computer and flashed up our presentation. By midnight, we had something that I thought would suffice. It wasn't fantastic, but it was the best we could do in such a short time.

Joni and I turned up for the appointment ready to rock. Even though we lacked a beautiful glossy dossier, we had some things going for us. We were hungry for business, and we knew our market well. We presented our fledgling plan with confidence, as though it were a high-powered and cohesive proposal. We gave it our all and promised to make the subdivision a success.

The developer thanked us and sent us on our way. He was interviewing several large companies with a whole lot more experience in new home sales throughout the day. Quite frankly, our chances looked slim. Nonetheless, all the way home, Joni and I jabbered on about how amazing it would be to secure a listing agreement for a subdivision of a few hundred homes. Our adrenaline was still pumping after our performance, and we were tingling just thinking about this farfetched possibility. It would be career changing, almost too good to be true. We had given it our best effort, and now we would have to wait. It would probably be a week or two until we heard our fate.

Larry called me the next day. Stunned astonishment probably best describes my reaction. He had chosen Joni and me as his new marketing and sales team for his new subdivision. He wanted us to meet his builder team. He wanted to set up a meeting with us immediately so we could get going on our new job. We had a contract to iron out. I was so overcome with excitement, I could hardly hear the words coming over the phone. I pinched myself a little as he kept talking. I was furiously trying to attract Joni's attention with wild arm-waving gestures and bizarre facial contortions. I turned my attention back to the phone conversation at hand. Yes! It was happening. We had secured the opportunity to sell an entire new subdivision. Not only that, but Larry was offering us the most generous terms imaginable. He was going to make sure we had all the resources we needed, and he agreed to compensate us extremely well. He anticipated that the build-out would take a few years of very hard work, but the job was ours if we were up to it.

I could hardly believe it. In real estate terms, this was the opportunity of a lifetime. I had only been selling real estate for a few months, had just started a new company a few weeks prior, and knew next to nothing about new construction. Yet here we were being offered the real estate jackpot. It was a miracle. I got off the phone and screamed one of the loudest screams I think I have ever screamed. I am sure it could be heard all the way across the country! Joni's head whipped up.

"Really?" she said in disbelief when I told her about our offer. "We got it? Really?" We started celebrating, whooping and hollering together in a most unladylike fashion. We hugged each other about fifty times and did more than a little jig. The insurance agents in the office next door thought we were nuts. The high-fives kept going all day long, confirmation to our neighbors that we were indeed as crazy as they suspected.

Years later, Larry, the developer, told me that he had taken a huge gamble on us. He said that when we came into his office that day, something about our presentation eclipsed the others. Our materials were not as glossy or slick, clearly our experience in new home sales was limited, but our determination and preparation had convinced him that we could do a great job. He said we connected with him. I will forever be grateful to Larry for having faith in us and giving us such an incredible opportunity. He truly was another angel in my journey, and he will always have a special place in my heart.

And so, the very next day, my new career took off to levels that I never could have anticipated. Joni and I worked so hard. It was one of those twenty-four seven situations, but I loved it. I had a fantastic team of builders, a developer providing brilliant guidance, and the economy was booming. I was on a steep learning curve, and I don't believe I have ever worked harder than I did during those first few years. I thrived. Our company boomed.

It was a time of great prosperity for us. We were very blessed with a good life. Everything seemed perfect. One day, as I was driving to my office, I remember quite clearly thinking, *I love my life. It is perfect.* I savored that moment. It was almost as if I wanted my life to stand still for that split second because everything was so freaking good. We were living the American dream. In a short few years, we had come a long way from the near-penniless immigrant family who laid down on the floor and pulled their coats over them for warmth. The scary decision to move to the US for an initial six months had developed into something I could have never in my wildest dreams have conjured. My thankfulness knew no limits.

CHAPTER 19

· · · · · · · · · · · · · · · · · ·

A Slow Unraveling and Never Say Never

North Carolina saw unparalleled growth and kept topping the charts as one of the best places in the United States to reside. However, the recession that had ravaged housing markets on the West Coast had begun to pummel home prices in our state as well. As we neared build-out of the large subdivision, I started to see homes fall into foreclosure. It was very distressing. I had many listing appointments where I gave bad news to homeowners who needed to sell. As their home values dramatically declined, their mortgages turned upside down. Home sales nosedived.

Murray continued working as a contractor. Unfortunately, he was now in a job that he did not enjoy at all, but with unemployment rocketing sky high, he could not seem to find anything better. He was going numb inside. He dreaded going to work and each day, he would drag himself out of the door with a sense of resignation. His cheery, fun-loving demeanor was waning. But without a new job to jump to, he couldn't just quit. We had some fairly large financial commitments. We had moved into a beautiful new home a few years back and still had a substantial mortgage to cover. Our daughters were in college, and that was another good-sized financial commitment.

So my ears perked up when he told me that the British company that had originally brought us to the US had a job opening for him. That was until he told me the job opportunity was in New York. The company's head office was now located on Wall Street. I heard a timbre in his voice I had not heard in a long time. He seemed so animated by the possibility of this job, but I was torn. I wanted him to have a job he enjoyed, but not in New York City, which was obviously far away from our home. I could not leave my business; it was our main source of revenue. The only alternative: Murray could commute to New York during the week and return home on the weekends. I hated the idea. Intensely.

He flew to New York on a reconnaissance trip. The interviews went well, and a job offer ensued. I hadn't seen him so excited in a long time. A new spark was lit inside of him. Despite the fact that I wanted Murray to be happier, I still hated this option.

When he told me that he was taking the new job, I cried. I did not want him to leave. He promised me we would spend every weekend together. He would either come home, or I could stay in our New York apartment with him. It didn't matter—I still cried.

As I watched him pack his suitcase, I distinctly remember thinking, *Our life is changing forever.* Deep inside, I just knew it.

I am a positive person. I got this from my father, who always saw the best in every situation. I mean always. No matter what happened in his life, he always found a bright side. It was the thing that I loved most about him. So I dug deep inside to find the positive, as my father would have done. But it did not come easily. By the time I dropped Murray off at the airport for the first week of his new job, I was determined to make the best of this unwelcome development. I resolved to go with the flow of this new shift in our lifestyle, despite the fact that I had a heavy heart. I would adapt. I would make it work.

In reality, I slowly began to unravel inside. I felt such emptiness without my soulmate beside me. I hated the separation. No matter what fabulous activities we planned for our weekends together, I did not enjoy them because I was unhappy with the overall situation. To top it off, Murray hates talking on phones. For some strange reason, this highly intelligent individual became a grunting, monosyllabic zombie on the end of the phone. Catching up with each other at the end of our very full days was never good. Although I couldn't wait to chat with him and tell him all about my day, I dreaded the calls. They were awful.

• • •

There is nothing like a little bit of adversity or discomfort intruding on your tranquility to make you sit up and take stock of things. It can make you stop and ask questions. "Meaning of life" type questions. This New York debacle did exactly that for me.

Suddenly, I saw my life with new eyes. I realized that somehow, over the past several years, I had become stuck on the treadmill of life. I was so busy chasing after a successful lifestyle that I was now running on autopilot. I could not remember the last time I really tuned in to my *inner voice*. I had left no time in my schedule to stop and listen.

This happens to many people. It sort of creeps up on each of us. We have great passion and deep meaning in life, and then we awake one day and find that it has all vanished.

I wondered what had happened to the passion I once had for helping others. It was something I loved doing. It was who I was. Why had I stopped? Had it been buried by my "busyness"? Had I lost my way as I built my American dream? The very essence of me had gone dull.

After several years of being a little deaf, I started to hear a whisper inside me again. Ever so quietly, something was stirring.

• • •

I always looked forward to my Friday evenings with Murray, especially when he returned to North Carolina. One particularly hot and steamy Friday night, we sat on our screened porch with a glass of lovely cabernet. Murray had just got in from New York, and we were winding down, chatting about our busy week. We loved to watch the fireflies glimmer and listen to the cacophony of the frogs down by the stream in the woods.

"It sounds like they're screaming bloody murder!" Murray would say when the frog song reached fever pitch, as it had on this sweltering hot night. I giggled over how predictable his comments were. We sat for some time in silence, just enjoying being together again.

"I think we should move to California," he uttered in a rather lackadaisical manner. I heard what sounded like loud, clanging cymbals inside me as these completely unpredictable words pierced through the thick night air and hit my brain.

"Why?" I asked casually, trying not to sound too surprised at his harebrained suggestion that had come totally out of left field. My heart had started going jumpity-jump. He had my attention, but I was not letting him know that just then. *Stay cool, Leanne*, I whispered to myself.

"I think we need a change." More clanging sounds! Where the hell had this come from? I wondered. I thought he loved his job in New York.

"I've been thinking about this a lot actually." He ploughed on. "We both love the ocean and the mountains, and we love being outdoors all year round. We should live somewhere that we love. You don't like the cold and I don't like the heat, so it would be great to live somewhere with a very temperate climate that we can both enjoy. Now that the girls have moved away, there's nothing really keeping us here."

Everything Murray was saying sort of made sense. But what about the business I had built up from scratch? I couldn't just leave that, could I? What about his job in New York? What about my beautiful dream home that we had only been living in for a few years? Should we just walk away from everything that was our current life? I guess our financial commitments had finally lessened. He was right that our daughters had both recently married and moved away from the area. But us moving too? Was he nuts?

Lately, I noticed he was showing signs of being a little worn out by his high-pressure job, as well as the weekly supercommute. I missed the fun-loving, quirky man that I married. On some of our weekends together, I secretly wondered if the spark may have started to seep out of our marriage. We both seemed so tired all the time. The thought of something new and different was nowhere on my radar. But when my kooky husband nonchalantly threw this suggestion out to me that evening, something inside me started to churn.

As I pondered the ramifications of this unexpected but totally exhilarating idea, thunder began to rumble in the night sky above us. Then a huge fork of lightning flashed across the sky and illuminated us. The heavens opened, and a deluge of driving rain exploded from above, splashing right through the screen and onto our couch.

As we skedaddled indoors, I remember thinking, *Here we go again!* I knew that voice when it spoke to me. It had been awhile since I had heard it, but I knew it loud and clear.

• • •

I was all tingly that weekend. I could not stop thinking about this preposterous notion that we should suddenly quit everything we were doing and start up somewhere else. Even though we had done this several times before in our lives, it seemed especially nuts this time. I thought we had finally settled down and stopped doing crazy.

"Never moving again!" were words that had passed my lips numerous times over the past few years. I had confidently announced this proclamation to all who cared to listen. I smiled to myself, because deep down I knew that every time I had said those words in the past, I was setting myself up for something new. *Never say never*, I thought for the hundredth time and did a big, fat eyeroll at myself.

Gradually, over that momentous weekend, Murray and I talked about this screwball idea. He knew I was not very happy with our living situation. It was wearing thin on him too. He felt it was time for a change. He had researched climates at locations that were near the beach. His analysis had pinpointed a stretch of coast from San Diego to San Francisco that fit his "ideal location." He figured that life was short, so we should make the most of it and enjoy where we live.

Well, that was true.

"You never cease to surprise me," I mentioned to him later that night. "I know we have never done things by the book, but this is definitely out there. Every time we have moved, it has turned out to be so right. I need to think this through. I feel that little 'yes buzz' inside of me that I can't seem to shake. As much as this idea of huge change again makes me nervous, I love that you are open to continually advancing and never letting life get stale. I love that you stretch my thinking to new possibilities." I thumped him on the arm for pushing my thinking out of its little comfy nest. Meanwhile, I thought a big, fat, humongous *Yikes!*

For the next week, I mulled over Murray's ridiculous moving idea. When he came home the following weekend, I announced, "I am going to put our home up for sale and see what happens." I was sure my pupils had just dilated to saucers. I could hardly believe it when I heard those words float out of my mouth so easily. I had surprised myself. This was the beautiful dream home that I had designed with our patient builder. I absolutely loved living here. Everything was perfect. It had taken me years to find the stunning lot. I had planted an acre of flower gardens, which were just starting to look resplendent. The pool sparkled at me every day when I jumped in it for a relaxing swim. From the vantage point of our bubbling hot tub, the night stars were particularly breathtaking. We were nestled on three acres of majestic mature woods with a stream running through, all just ten minutes from downtown Chapel Hill. It was my little slice of paradise. I loved coming home every day to this elegant French Country home with its beautiful craftsmanship and peaceful living spaces. We had only been living here for five years, but we had built it as our "stay forever" home.

We were right in the middle of a big recession. House prices had plummeted since we had built our home. The market was so sluggish that I was certain our house probably wouldn't sell for its listing price. If we were able to sell it in this depressed market, it would be a definitive indicator regarding our foolhardy "move across the country to the unknown" idea.

A couple of weeks later, after much fluffing and buffing of my palace, I grabbed a mallet, drove down to our mailbox, and pounded a "For Sale" sign into the baked red soil. Gulp!

We had planned a short trip to visit Julia and her husband, who were living in Wisconsin. Murray was flying from New York, and I was flying from Raleigh. We would meet up in Madison. I was scheduled to depart the day after the momentous mallet-pounding event. I did not expect much interest in our house in such a sluggish economic climate, but the pets would be gone and the house would be empty and easy for agents to show.

Before I could get out of town, the phone started blowing up with showing requests. By the time I was boarding the flight to Madison, we had received a great offer on our house. I was stunned. Our house had just sold for a fantastic price during a terrible recession while I was sitting on a plane! I had become so used to telling my clients that there was no way they could sell their house for what they hoped it was worth, but here I was accepting a ridiculously good offer on my country estate. It all seemed rather surreal. Even more astonishing: I felt ecstatic about what had just transpired in the last few hours. I had expected to feel sad to leave my beloved abode, but strangely I did not.

As I disembarked in Madison and ran to hug my beautiful daughter, I realized that we had now created a new problem for ourselves. We had no idea where we were heading. We had no idea if we would make it out to the West Coast, to be frank. We knew no one there. In fact, we weren't even sure exactly where "there" was. Nonetheless, I had an overwhelming sense of inner peace with what we had just done.

• • •

Hurricane Sandy hit the East Coast on the day I said goodbye to my dream home. Gale force winds and monsoonlike rains buffeted us as we woke up for the last time in our now empty house. I rolled out of the airbed onto the floor and looked over at our cat and dog hunkered down together on the dog's bed. I announced to Murray and the pets, "Let the adventure begin!" Our cat, Prissy, gave me a haunting yowl. She knew change was afoot.

Murray was meant to fly back to New York on the early morning flight, but all flights into and out of New York were canceled. His office on Wall Street had closed its doors for a brief time due to damage, flooding, and power outages in lower Manhattan. I was so thankful to unexpectedly have him at my side so that I didn't have to say goodbye to our home alone. We bundled the thoroughly disgruntled pets into the car and headed for the attorney's office. Debris was flying everywhere as we drove through inches of water.

No looking back, I whispered to myself. This was real!

We signed the papers and drove directly to our daughter Victoria and her husband's home. It was four hours away on the Outer Banks of North Carolina. They had offered to care for our cat and dog while we were homeless and figuring out our next move. Everything had moved so quickly that we had got no further in our planning than the sale of our home.

Lashed by wind, rain, lightning and thunder, Murray and I were a little pensive as we listened to the whoosh of our car's frenzied windshield wipers while we dodged large branches strewn along the highway. Weather this powerful was a little reminder to let the bigness of life happen. The past few weeks had been one hell of a whirlwind. But even then, we knew this was the right decision.

With our cat howling even louder than the wind outside, and our carsick dog shaking uncontrollably, we drove through water up to our car doors to reach our destination.

Only six weeks ago, we had been sitting on our porch on a balmy evening, talking about crazy change. And here we were, temporarily homeless, wondering where the heck we were headed next. We still had no plan. Just a few days earlier when one of the movers had asked where we were moving to, I'd said that I really had no idea. The man had looked at me like I was insane, so I had demurely suggested he give me a quote for keeping everything in storage in North Carolina for a few months (because that's where I still had my business), a quote to move everything to New York (because that's where Murray still had his job), and a quote to move to California.

He then asked me, "Where in California, because you do know, ma'am, it is a big state." My honest answer was, "Sir, I have absolutely no idea!"

No, I was not your normal customer. But at least I was not staying stuck in a rut. I was coming alive again, and I was excited and terrified all at the same freaking time.

CHAPTER 20

· · · · · · · · · · · · · · · · · · ·

Heading West and Finding Shangri-la

Thanksgiving weekend was just four weeks away. It would be an ideal time to take a few days off and fly to California to explore the possibilities. After all, this notion of heading West was what had started this whole wild expedition. It was time to see what was really out there.

We certainly knew that we couldn't stay in limbo for long. I was temporarily gatecrashing at the home of a kind friend in Raleigh and was still buried up to my eyeballs in my thriving business. Murray remained in New York, stressed to the hilt with his job. We needed to make some big decisions fast, so we planned our reconnaissance trip. We would drive up the coast and stop at the places that had made their way onto Murray's "possibly perfect location" list. We loved road trips.

We flew into San Diego and had a week to get up to San Francisco before returning to New York. We had no fixed itinerary, except to bypass Los Angeles, because big cities are just not our thing. It was a truly spectacular drive up the coast. The warmth and beauty of California acted as a tonic to our souls. It was fantastic to be together again for an entire week. It made me feel alive to my very core.

As we drove into Santa Barbara I asked Murray why we were stopping there for the night. I knew nothing at all about the town. Murray mentioned something about "south facing means lots of sun all day, perfect climate for us, might be interesting." None of this really got my attention, but by the following day we had fallen in love with this gem. Words can't describe the beauty of this small Riviera-style town nestled between the azure Pacific Ocean and the majestic mountains. It made my soul sing to be there. We stayed another night, and my heart swelled with the feeling of coming home. Weird, I know, but that is really what happened. I was full of a sense of belonging. That quiet *inner voice* spoke to me. I took note.

By the end of a most wonderful week driving up the coast, we looked at each other and emphatically said without a spot of doubt, "Let's move to Santa Barbara."

Whaaaat?

Logically, there was a myriad of reasons why this move was crazy. We knew no one there; we had no job possibilities waiting for us; we had limited resources; and we had no real plan of what we would do once we got there. However, we did have a very good reason to make this choice. We knew deep within us that this was what we needed to do. We had experienced the same profound conviction many times before. Every time we made a move, we had known above all else that it was the right choice for us. Whenever it seemed implausible or even impossible, we had seen miracles unfold when they were needed the most. Even though it had been awhile since we had taken such a big step, we were sure things would open up for us and that everything would work out as it had done before.

Or so we thought . . .

• • •

At the beginning of December, we arrived back in New York, ecstatic to have a plan. I zipped back down to North Carolina. Our town hosted an annual Christmas parade the first weekend in December. We always threw our company holiday party on the same day because the parade went right past our office. Every year, hundreds of clients and friends would drop in to watch the festivities and join in the celebrations. It was always incredibly merry.

This year, our holiday fete also became my impromptu farewell party. It felt strange to hear myself say goodbye to all the people who had been a part of my life for the past decade and a half. I could hardly believe my own ears when I revealed to my perplexed acquaintances that I was moving to Santa Barbara. Given my own incredulity, it was no wonder they were a little baffled. When questioned why, my only answer was, "It's time for us to make a change." Understandably, reactions spanned the spectrum from "You are a complete and utter lunatic"(expressed in an infinitely more polite Southern way of course) to "I wish I could do something like that."

Later that night, I returned to my friend's home, where I was still interloping for a couple more weeks. We chatted about following our dreams. As we talked, I had a fresh awareness that every single person alive can be true to himself or herself and follow that thing they know is for them to do in this life. In fact, it is why we are here on earth.

• • •

The day before Christmas, I signed the documents to sell my business, and Murray flew back from New York for the last time to meet me in Chapel Hill. He was not the slightest bit sad to close the door on his New York apartment and hand the keys back to the landlord. We were ready for the journey ahead. We drove to my daughter's home to pick up our dog and enjoy family Christmas celebrations. Our cat would stay with Victoria, as she was just too old to move across the country.

Murray did his packing trick once again. After all these years, he still had the magic. Somehow he had apparently waved his wizard's wand over our remaining chattels. Miraculously, he fit what looked like a busload full of stuff into our small SUV and still left room for the dog and me to squeeze in. At the crack of dawn on New Year's Day, we set off on our road trip. Our drive would take us from the Atlantic Ocean on the East Coast to the Pacific Ocean on the West Coast, a distance of about 3,000 miles.

What are we unleashing? I wondered as we drove past the North Carolina state line.

I looked at our scaredy-cat dog, Dalia, who hated car rides. She huddled in a tiny spot behind me and shook uncontrollably. I turned and gave her a big hug. As I patted her precious, quivering head, I was excited *and* terrified by what we were doing: moving across the country to the unknown, just because we believed it was what we were meant to do next! "Are we crazy?" I asked Murray and Dalia, not for the first or last time, as a big doggy drool slopped down my back.

I thought of the quote by Voltaire: "Faith consists in believing when it is beyond the power of reason to believe." There was no "reason" to do what we were doing, just a deep inner sense that this is what we needed to do. That voice inside us yelling "YES!"

Five days later, we rolled into Santa Barbara on a grey and drizzly day. Wide-eyed, Murray and I looked at each other and asked, "Now what?"

• • •

I would love to tell you a fairytale version of what happened next: We found good jobs right away, bought a lovely new house to replace the beautiful one we had left behind, and lived happily ever after, totally fulfilled and enjoying the good life in paradise.

The part about living in paradise is absolutely true. Santa Barbara is my Shangri-la. I have a deep, heartfelt gratitude for the beauty of the environment that I live in. I am eternally thankful to daily walk my dog on the beach while chatting to my kind and gentle husband. I love exploring the mountains on magnificent hikes. I have found a culture in which I truly belong and have made many sincerely amazing friends in a very short time. I have come home.

But the truth is that we did not find jobs right away, and therefore we could not buy a house. Santa Barbara is an expensive place to live. For the first couple of years, we pushed on doors that banged shut. We embarked on a few business ventures that fell through. Our limited resources quickly dwindled. I will never forget the day that my husband quietly said to me, "We need to talk." He told me that we were basically destitute. It was a terrifying moment. I felt as though I could not breathe and that my heart had stopped.

This was not how it was meant to go.

I was downright terrified right to my very core.

Many nights, I would awake in an absolute panic, racked by sheer terror. By day, as silly as this may seem, I hated walking past homeless people in town, because in my mind there was a stark possibility that I could become one of them if something did not change very soon. We had thrown all caution to the wind and followed our inner voice, yet things were not looking good. We had totally run out of resources. We not only had a bank balance of zero, but we had depleted our retirement savings and were carrying heavy debt. It was so overwhelming that I did not know where to turn or what to do.

I could not believe that we had arrived at this point. Understandably, I became very angry with my husband and myself. We were in our early fifties, when most people were thinking of retirement. Instead, we had to figure out how to pay our rent and how to buy basic groceries each week. We sold as many belongings as we could and worked as hard as possible to try and remedy our dire situation. It was a very dark time. We were trying to claw our way out of a deep hole. I felt stuck in my worst nightmare. One of my greatest fears, total financial ruin, had engulfed me.

For months, I was immersed in terrible inner turmoil and found myself lashing out at Murray and considering running far away from him and our situation. I wanted my life to be different. I did not want "hard." I wanted "easy." I wanted it fixed. Slowly, because I had hit rock bottom and had nowhere else to turn, I began to ask myself, "What am I meant to be learning?" Funny how that happens. We often need to get below empty for some new truth to awaken inside of us.

Could it be that I was meant to have arrived at this point? Was there something more important than having a life that was always happy, easy, and stable? Was there a purpose to our loss? I needed a deep inner shift, and perhaps this was the only possible way for it to take place.

I listened to my inner voice, and the message was loud and clear: It was time to stop wishing things were different. What was done was done, and no amount of wishing could change the position I was now in. It was time to stop doubting the decisions that had put me where I was at this point in my life. We believed that we were meant to take this path, so there must be a reason it had taken us to this difficult place.

It was certainly time to stop being angry and blaming my husband and myself. Blame is a destructive response to adversity. It was time to put that emotion to an end. It was also time to stop projecting over and over in my mind all the worst-case scenarios that could ensue. That was a total waste of time, and it just resulted in more deep, unnecessary fear.

Instead, I had to accept my life situation as it was right then and there. It was time to enjoy the "now moment," rather than imagining a terrible future as a destitute and hopeless individual. I had to shift my paradigm. I realized that even though one part of my life sucked, I could still enjoy it. My loss did not define me. In essence, it was about my attitude, not my circumstances. I may have lost some things, but I still had an abundance of other things to be thankful for. Why not focus on those things instead? Our financial ruin may have knocked me down, but I was not out.

During the last few years of living in North Carolina, I had lost hold of the vibrant power I had once known in my life. I had become dull inside and purposeless in some ways.

Now, as a result of this awful ordeal in California, I was on the cusp of exciting new things. I could not see a damn thing yet, but I knew, because I just knew, that good things would soon open up. I had hope. Things had clearly not gone the way I had expected. It was time to open my heart and mind to something new. I had no idea what that would be, but I knew it would be perfect for me. I had faith in miracles. I had faith again in the power of things unseen.

ABOUT THE AUTHOR

· · · · · · · · · · · · · · · · · ·

Leanne R Wood is a spirited trailblazer, business entrepreneur, author, and keynote speaker. She has lived in New Zealand, Switzerland, Ireland, Canada, England, Scotland, Romania and the USA. Her raw honesty, deep passion, ability to laugh at things, and heartfelt communication skills have been honed by following her intuition and listening to her *inner voice*. Leanne has  two daughters and a granddaughter. She resides with her lifelong fellow adventurer and husband, Murray, in Santa Barbara.

Morgan James
Speakers Group

www.TheMorganJamesSpeakersGroup.com

We connect Morgan James published authors with live and online events and audiences whom will benefit from their expertise.

 Morgan James makes all of our titles available
through the Library for All Charity Organization.

www.LibraryForAll.org